Visual Guide to Math

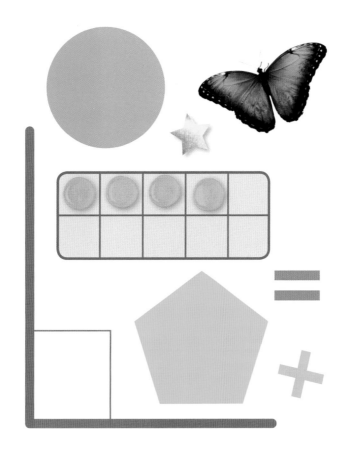

Written by Karen Wilding
Senior editors Jolyon Goddard, Cécile Landau
Senior art editor Ann Cannings
Project art editor Emma Hobson
US senior editor Shannon Beatty
US editor Elizabeth Searcy
Art editor Shipra Jain
Editorial assistance Marie Greenwood,
Carrie Love, Kathleen Teece
Additional design Dave Ball
DTP designers Rajesh Singh, Vijay Kandwal
Senior DTP designer Shanker Prasad
Jacket coordinator Francesca Young
Jacket designer Dheeraj Arora
Managing editor Laura Gilbert
Managing art editor Diane Peyton Jones
Preproducer Nadine King
Producer Basia Ossowska
Creative director Helen Senior
Publishing director Sarah Larter

Math consultant Meryl Glicksman

First American edition, 2018
Published in the United States by DK Publishing
345 Hudson Street, New York, New York 10014

A catalog record for this book is available from the Library of Congress.
ISBN: 978-1-4654-7093-5

DK books are available at special discounts when purchased in bulk
for sales promotions, premiums, fund-raising, or educational use.
For details, contact: DK Publishing Special Markets, 345 Hudson Street,
New York, New York 10014
SpecialSales@dk.com

Printed and bound in China

A WORLD OF IDEAS:
SEE ALL THERE IS TO KNOW

www.dk.com

Contents

Introduction

Visual Guide to Math gives your children the key skills necessary to be confident in using math, not only at school but also in many of their everyday activities.

Making math fun

Many children struggle with math. They fail to understand what numbers really are and how they relate to the world around them. This book takes a fresh, fun approach, using simple visual tools to show, as well as tell, children how math works.

Key topics

By working through this book, your child will learn about the following:

- Numbers and counting
- Patterns
- Comparison
- Addition and subtraction
- Multiplication and division
- Measurements
- Shapes
- Data, tables, and graphs

Headings tell you the topic you're about to explore.

Comparing

We often **compare** the sizes of thing or lengths. We can use words and s\ are **more than**, **less than**, or **equal t**

Using bars

We can use bars to show the things we are comparing and use symbols instead of wor

Color photography helps link math ideas to the real world.

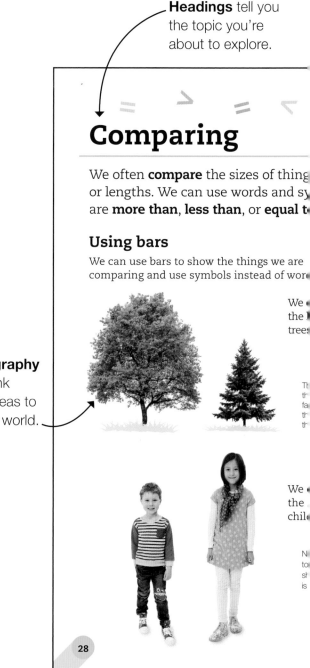

We the tree

Th th fa th th

We the chil

N to sh is

How the book works

Each page or pair of pages explores either a new topic or takes you a step further into an area of math covered earlier in the book. You can dip in and out, but the book works best when you work through the pages in order.

Keys facts
are highlighted.

Tabs tell you the math skills covered.

Illustrated examples make math concepts clearer and easier to grasp.

Visual tools, such as grids, ten frames, and number lines, boost understanding.

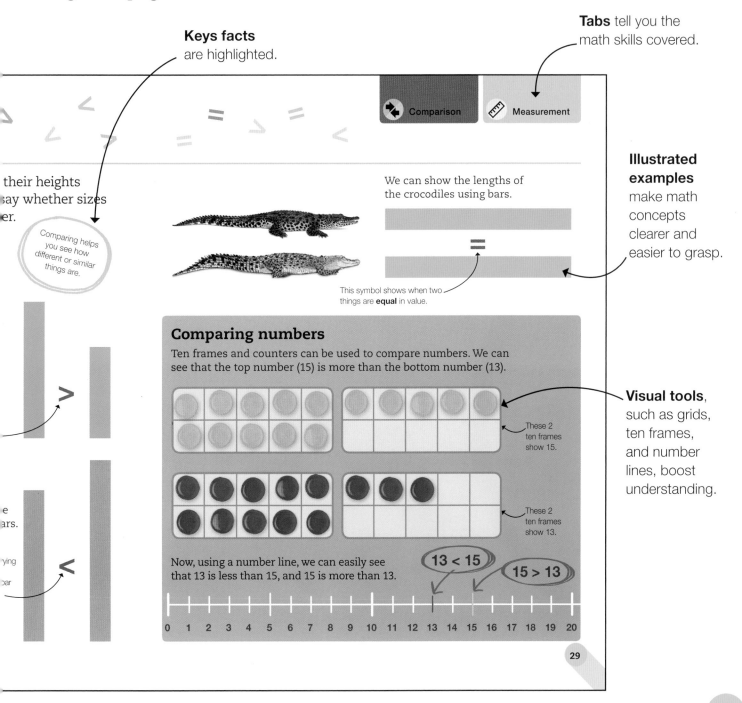

Comparison   Measurement

their heights
say whether sizes
er.

Comparing helps you see how different or similar things are.

We can show the lengths of the crocodiles using bars.

This symbol shows when two things are **equal** in value.

Comparing numbers

Ten frames and counters can be used to compare numbers. We can see that the top number (15) is more than the bottom number (13).

These 2 ten frames show 15.

These 2 ten frames show 13.

Now, using a number line, we can easily see that 13 is less than 15, and 15 is more than 13.

13 < 15   15 > 13

0 1 2 3 4 5 6 7 8 9 10 11 12 13 14 15 16 17 18 19 20

29

What is math?

Math is all around you. Math is numbers, counting, patterns, shapes, calculations, fractions, and much, much more. Everything in our world involves math.

Where do you use math in your everyday life?

Learning math at school helps us solve everyday problems and organize our lives. Whether we are playing a game, drawing a picture, or spending money, we use math skills to do these tasks.

Measuring distance

We use math when we measure distances with a ruler or tape measure.

Telling time involves math skills.

Using money

Measuring temperature

Knowing what time it is

Counting, saving, and spending money all use math.

We use math to check how hot or cold something is with a thermometer.

Weighing things

We use math to
weigh ingredients.

When we divide up
a cake to share,
we use math.

Dividing a cake into equal parts

Using math for work

Every job that grown-ups do uses math.
Good math skills make your work easier.

A chef uses math to measure
ingredients for a recipe.

Doctors and nurses use math to figure
out the amount of medicine to give.

A builder uses
math to figure out
how big something
needs to be.

Numbers everywhere!

Have you noticed numbers around you? There are numbers everywhere we look. Have you ever thought about why they are there?

Phones

Phones have numbers to press or tap, so you can put in a phone number and talk to someone.

Watches and clocks

The numbers 1 to 12 are often seen on watches and clocks. They let you know what time it is.

Around the house

Look around your home. You might see numbers on the doors or walls, the refrigerator, the stove, and many other things.

Is there an apartment or house number on your front door?

License plates

Numbers are mixed up with letters on the license plates of cars, trucks, and other vehicles.

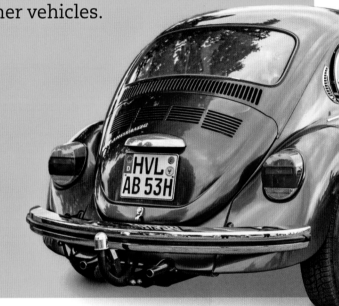

Compass

Numbers around the edge of a compass help you find directions more easily.

Road and street signs

Signs along roads often have numbers on them. They might tell you speed limits, distances, or the times of day when certain rules apply for road users.

Counting

We count to find out how many of something there are. This amount is called the **quantity**. We also count to figure out the **order** of a set of objects, such as which one is first, second, third, and so on.

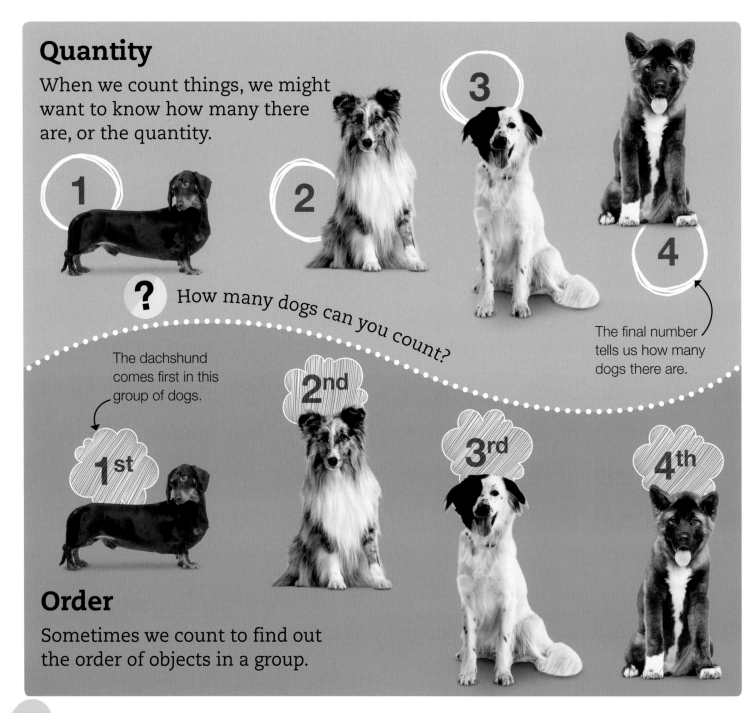

Quantity

When we count things, we might want to know how many there are, or the quantity.

? How many dogs can you count?

The final number tells us how many dogs there are.

The dachshund comes first in this group of dogs.

Order

Sometimes we count to find out the order of objects in a group.

There's more to counting...

Sometimes counting is a little more complicated. Look at the red and yellow counters below. Imagine that you just want to count the red ones. Here's how you do it.

1 You need to be able to see which counters are red.

2 You don't need to count any yellow counters.

3 Touch each red counter only once, and say what number it is (1, 2, 3, and so on) as you touch it.

4 Count all the red ones. Don't miss any.

5 You can count them in any order. You should always get the same number.

6 The last number you say tells you how many there are.

Math words for order

Here are some words that describe number order. What comes after **eleventh**?

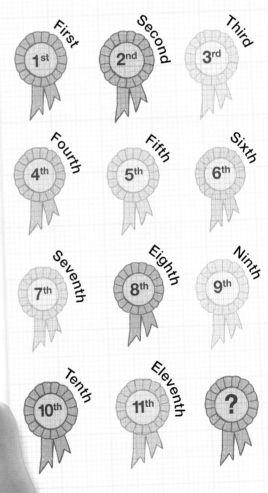

First — 1st
Second — 2nd
Third — 3rd
Fourth — 4th
Fifth — 5th
Sixth — 6th
Seventh — 7th
Eighth — 8th
Ninth — 9th
Tenth — 10th
Eleventh — 11th
?

Answer: Twelfth (12th)

Number order

We usually use symbols, such as 1, 3, 5, and 7, when we write numbers. Numbers follow an **order**, which can go up or down.

The order of the digits can tell us which number comes next.

Number symbols

The symbols for numbers are used all around the world. They are called **digits**. We put digits together to make other numbers, such as 24 or 107.

0	1	2	3	4	5	6	7	8	9
Zero	One	Two	Three	Four	Five	Six	Seven	Eight	Nine

Once we've learned the order that numbers go in, we can find a missing number.

1 2 3 4 5 6 (?) 8

The missing number is 7.

The order of the numbers can go up or down, and we don't always have to begin with 1.

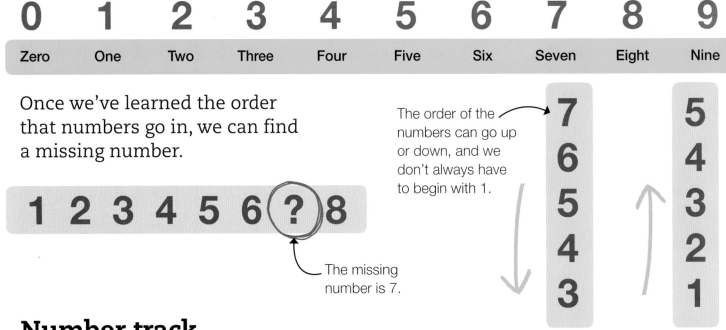

7
6
5
4
3

5
4
3
2
1

Number track

To help us understand number order, we can use a **number track**. On the track, each space is numbered. Each number can be matched with an object, so we can count the objects easily.

Each counter is matched with a number.

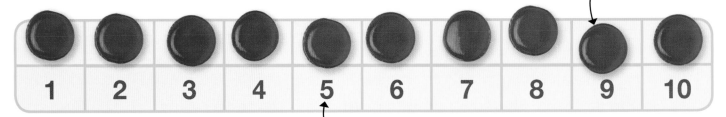

1	2	3	4	5	6	7	8	9	10

Each space has a number.

100s chart

Instead of just making a number track longer and longer, we can chop it up into groups of 10 to make a picture called a **100s chart**. 100s charts are useful for seeing patterns in numbers (see page 65).

1	2	3	4	5	6	7	8	9	10
11	12	13	14	15	16	17	18	19	20
21	22	23	24	25	26	27	28	29	30
31	32	33	34	35	36	37	38	39	40
41	42	43	44	45	46	47	48	49	50
51	52	53	54	55	56	57	58	59	60
61	62	63	64	65	66	67	68	69	70
71	72	73	74	75	76	77	78	79	80
81	82	83	84	85	86	87	88	89	90
91	92	93	94	95	96	97	98	99	100

Each line has 10 numbers.

The last line ends at 100, which is 10 groups of 10.

Seeing without counting

Your brain is amazing! Just by looking, you can often see how many things there are in a group **without counting** them. Practice doing this. It will help you become great at math.

How many peas?

Let's practice seeing without counting. Look at the peas on the plate.

? How did you see the peas? Did you see 4 peas at once without counting them, or did you see them in a different way?

Can you see another way of breaking up 4 on the opposite page?

Four can be broken up in different ways, as shown below.

4 peas

2 peas and **2** peas

3 peas and **1** pea

1 pea and **1** pea and **1** pea and **1** pea

Numbers in numbers

Every number is made up of other numbers. You're now learning to break up numbers and see numbers within numbers!

Instead of peas, let's now use squares.

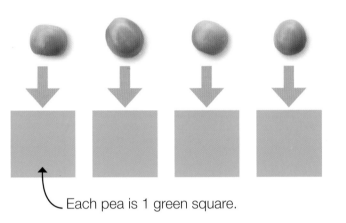

Each pea is 1 green square.

 👍 Practice looking at the squares and seeing the number without counting. This skill will help you work with numbers more easily.

Let's make the squares different colors to see the numbers that make up 4.

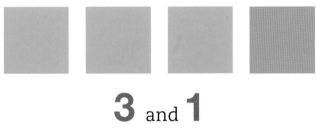

3 and **1**

1 and **1** and **1** and **1**

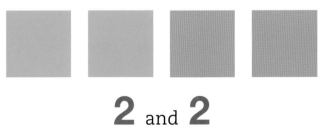

2 and **2**

1 and **2** and **1**

🔍 Can you see that 3 and 1 are parts of 4...
... and 2 and 2 are equal parts of 4?

Number patterns

Using number **patterns** helps you see how many of something there are without actually counting each one.

Making patterns

Let's look at ways of showing 8 with counters. We will start by using our fingers. Then we will use counters alone to show the number as patterns.

Patterns help us see numbers inside numbers.

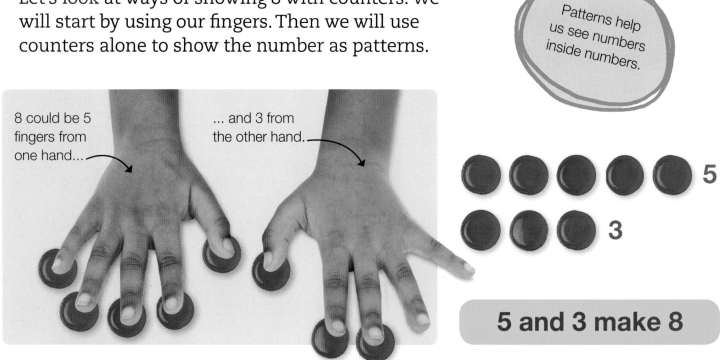

8 could be 5 fingers from one hand...

... and 3 from the other hand.

5

3

5 and 3 make 8

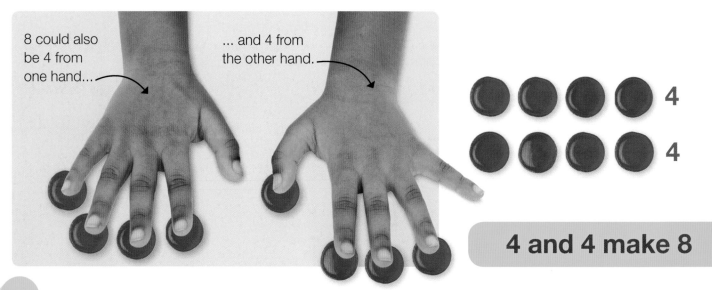

8 could also be 4 from one hand...

... and 4 from the other hand.

4

4

4 and 4 make 8

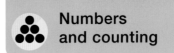

Patterns inside patterns

Arranging objects into tidy patterns makes it easier to see the smaller numbers inside bigger numbers.

Here are some cups. It's difficult to see how many there are without counting each one.

Let's arrange the cups into a tidy pattern. We can now see that there are 6 cups.

This is a pattern of 6 cups.

We can also see smaller number patterns inside the pattern of 6, including patterns of 2 and 3.

Pattern of 2

Pattern of 3

17

Ten-frame number patterns

A **ten frame** can be used to show numbers as patterns. The same numbers have **different patterns**, depending on how the frame is filled.

A **ten frame** is a grid with 10 squares.

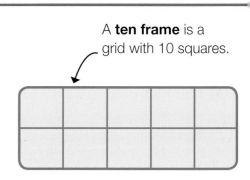

Making a ten frame

This is a number track. 10 counters are arranged along a line from 1 to 10.

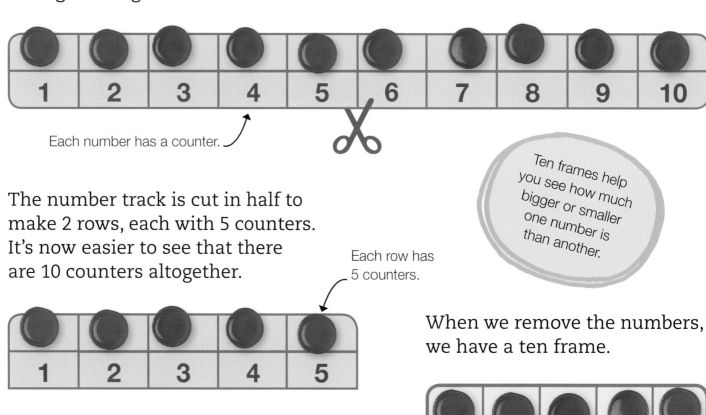

Each number has a counter.

The number track is cut in half to make 2 rows, each with 5 counters. It's now easier to see that there are 10 counters altogether.

Each row has 5 counters.

Ten frames help you see how much bigger or smaller one number is than another.

When we remove the numbers, we have a ten frame.

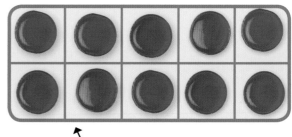

When a ten frame is filled, it shows a pattern of 10.

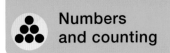
1 to 10

Let's show the numbers 1 to 10 on a ten frame. We'll make patterns by first filling the top 5 spaces on the ten frame, from left to right, and then the bottom 5 spaces.

To show numbers bigger than 10, you use more than one ten frame.

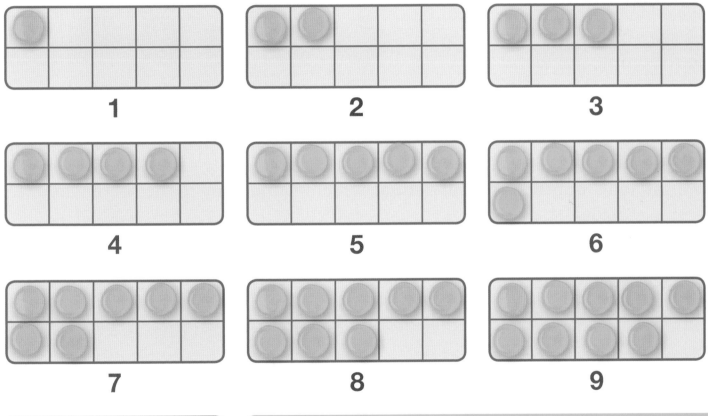

1

2

3

4

5

6

7

8

9

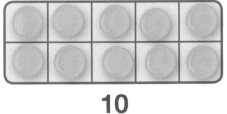

10

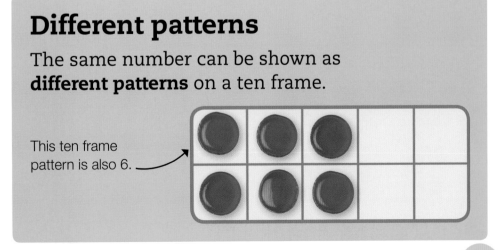

Different patterns

The same number can be shown as **different patterns** on a ten frame.

This ten frame pattern is also 6.

Numbers within numbers

By learning to see the different **patterns** in a number, we begin to see how that number can be split up into **other numbers**.

What other numbers can you see in 10?

Ten frames

We can use a **ten frame** to help us see ways of splitting, or **partitioning**, numbers.

We can look for groups that are **equal**, which means they're the same amount.

5 and 5 make 10

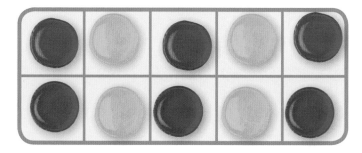

2 and 2 and 2 and 2 and 2 make 10

We can also partition into 2 or more unequal groups.

6 and 4 make 10

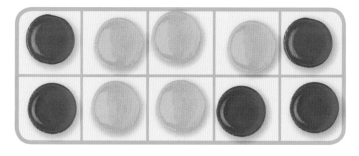

2 and 5 and 3 make 10

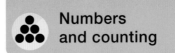
Arrays

An **array** is an arrangement of objects into horizontal lines, called **rows,** and vertical lines, called **columns**. We can see other numbers in arrays, as we do in ten frames.

In an array, all rows are equal in size, and all columns are also equal in size.

Look at the strawberries in this **array.**

Each column of this array has 3 strawberries.

Each row of this array has 4 strawberries.

Using counters to stand for strawberries, we can put them on ten frames. We now see that there is 1 group of 10, with 2 counters in the next ten frame, making 12.

10 and 2 make 12

The number 10

Our counting system is called a base-10 system because it is based on the **number 10**. When we finish a whole group of 10, we start another by adding 1, 2, 3, and so on until we have another group of 10.

Why 10?

Humans have been grouping things into 5s and 10s for thousands of years. This may be because each hand has 5 fingers.

5 and 5 make 10

1

5

2

4

3

Recording numbers

One of the earliest ways of recording groups of objects was by using **tally marks**. Each mark stands for 1 thing. When we have 5 things, the fifth line is drawn diagonally to show that the group is finished.

Using a counting system based on the number 10 makes it easy to count large groups.

1   2   3   4   5   6

Groups of 10

Many things we use in everyday life have scales showing groups of 10. We use these scales to help us measure things. The ruler you might use at school uses a scale. You can also see groups of 10 on the scales of thermometers and devices used for weighing.

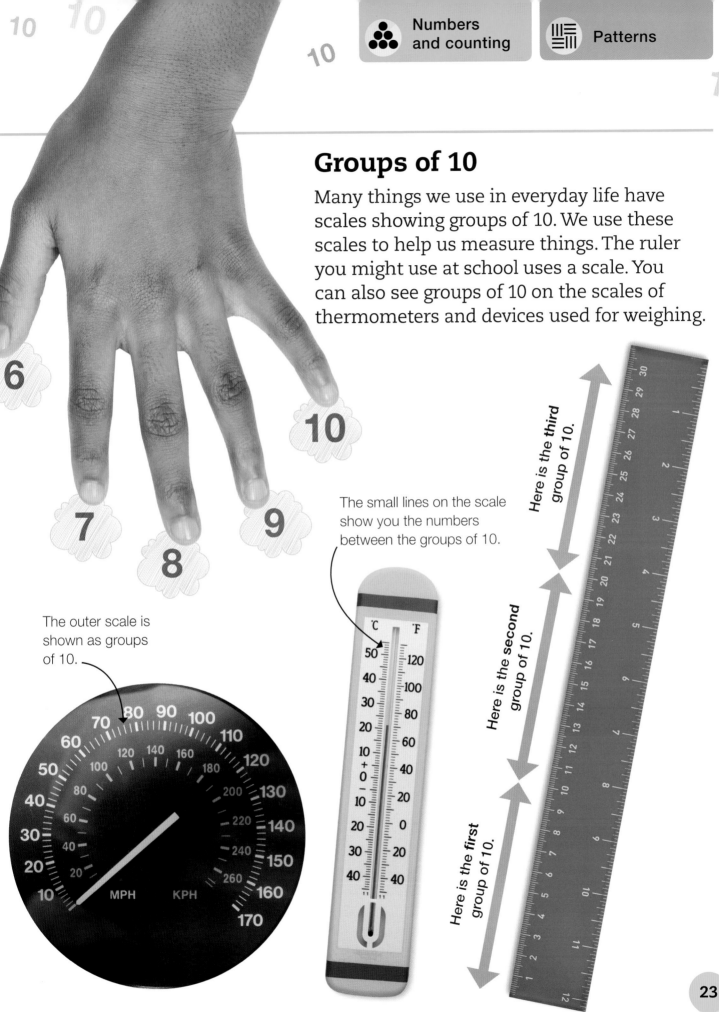

6

7

8

9

10

The small lines on the scale show you the numbers between the groups of 10.

Here is the third group of 10.

Here is the second group of 10.

Here is the first group of 10.

The outer scale is shown as groups of 10.

Number lines

A ten frame helps us see whole and partial groups of 10 in any number. In the real world, however, we often see these groups on **number lines**.

Number lines around us

You will see number lines on rulers, clocks, thermometers, weighing scales, and many more items.

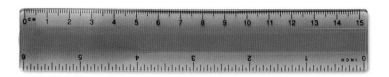

Making the connection

Let's now connect a number, shown on a ten frame, to its place on a number line.

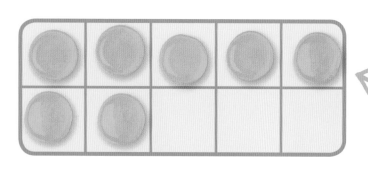

We see this 7 without counting, because it's 5 and 2. We can also see that it's 3 fewer than 10.

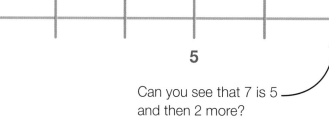

0   5   10

Can you see that 7 is 5 and then 2 more?

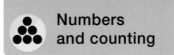
Bigger numbers

Here are **35** and **23** shown on ten frames and number lines.

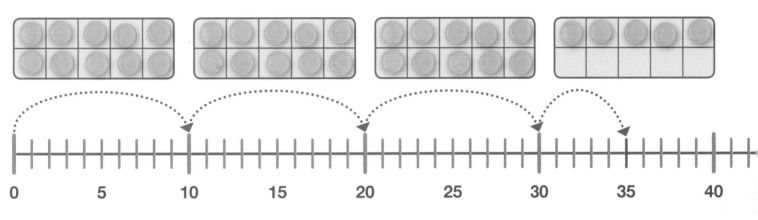

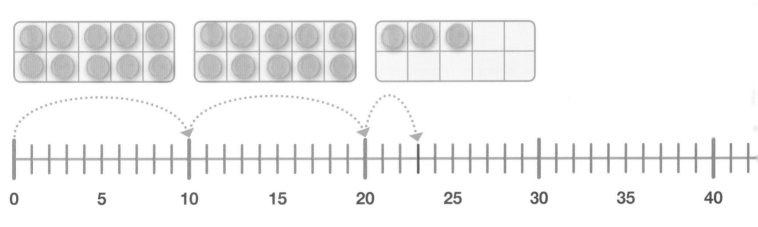

Looking at a number line

We can use a number line to see the difference in the size of numbers.

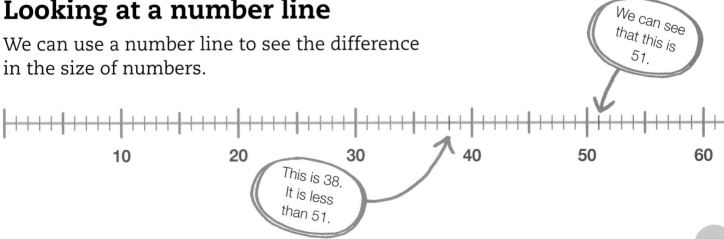

We can see that this is 51.

This is 38. It is less than 51.

Place value

Numbers 0 to 9 are written with just one digit, while numbers 10 and above have more. The value of each digit in a number depends on its place, or position, in the number.

Tens and ones

In numbers between 10 and 99, the first digit shows how many groups of 10 there are. The next digit shows groups of 1.

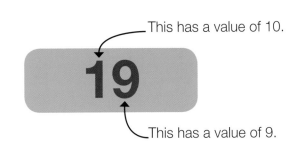

This has a value of 10.

This has a value of 9.

Using ten frames

Ten frames can be used to show how place value works with numbers over 10, such as 19.

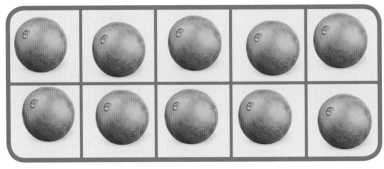

10 grapes

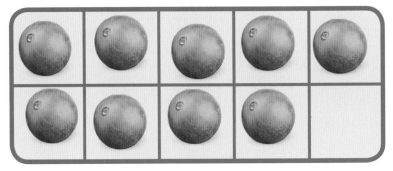

9 grapes

This tells you there is 1 group of 10 grapes.

19

This tells you there are 9 grapes in the next 10.

Number line

We can then show the same number of grapes on a number line.

1 group of 10 and then 9.

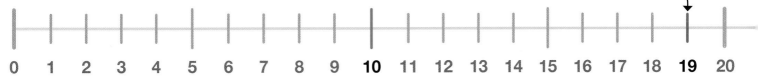

| 0 | 1 | 2 | 3 | 4 | 5 | 6 | 7 | 8 | 9 | **10** | 11 | 12 | 13 | 14 | 15 | 16 | 17 | 18 | **19** | 20 |

This complete line tells you there are 10 grapes.

100s chart

We can also show 19 on a 100s chart.

This line tells you there are 9 more grapes, making a total of 19 grapes.

1	2	3	4	5	6	7	8	9	10
11	12	13	14	15	16	17	18	19	20
21	22	23	24	25	26	27	28	29	30
31	32	33	34	35	36	37	38	39	40
41	42	43	44	45	46	47	48	49	50
51	52	53	54	55	56	57	58	59	60
61	62	63	64	65	66	67	68	69	70
71	72	73	74	75	76	77	78	79	80
81	82	83	84	85	86	87	88	89	90
91	92	93	94	95	96	97	98	99	100

A 100s chart is useful for seeing the place values in larger numbers.

Comparing

We often **compare** the sizes of things, such as their heights or lengths. We can use words and symbols to say whether sizes are **more than**, **less than**, or **equal to** each other.

Comparing helps you see how different or similar things are.

Using bars

We can use bars to show the things we are comparing and use symbols instead of words.

We can compare the heights of the trees using bars.

The open "mouth" of this symbol always faces the amount that it is **more than** the other.

>

We can compare the heights of the children using bars.

Now the "mouth" is trying to "eat" the right bar, showing that the left bar is **less than** the right.

<

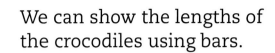
We can show the lengths of the crocodiles using bars.

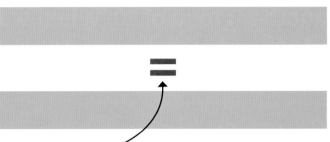

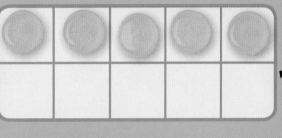

This symbol shows when two things are **equal** in value.

Comparing numbers

Ten frames and counters can be used to compare numbers. We can see that the top number (15) is more than the bottom number (13).

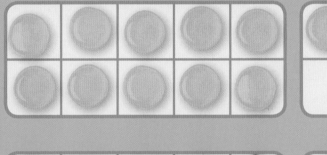

These 2 ten frames show 15.

These 2 ten frames show 13.

Now, using a number line, we can easily see that 13 is less than 15, and 15 is more than 13.

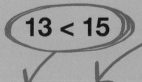

13 < 15

15 > 13

0 1 2 3 4 5 6 7 8 9 10 11 12 13 14 15 16 17 18 19 20

Making 100

Our counting system is based on the number 10. When we have counted one group of 10, we start counting another group of 10. When we have counted 10 groups of 10, we have reached **100**.

Counting big numbers

Instead of using ten frames to count a large amount of buttons, let's count them in groups of 10 and put each group in its own cup.

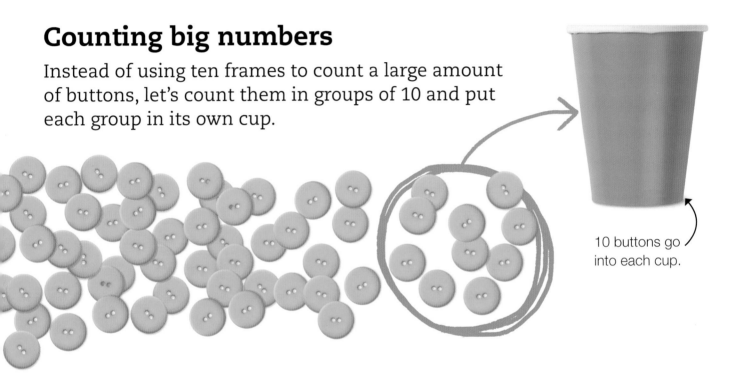

10 buttons go into each cup.

First we fill 9 cups. Each cup holds 10 buttons, so there are 90 buttons in cups.

Now we put 9 buttons into a tenth cup. We then have 99 buttons in cups. If we add another button to the tenth cup, we have made 10 groups of 10, which is **100**.

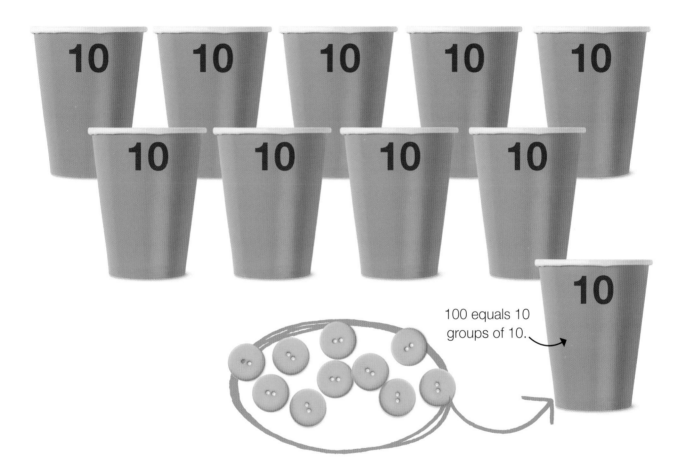

100 equals 10 groups of 10.

Number line

We can also show the amount in the filled cups on a number line.

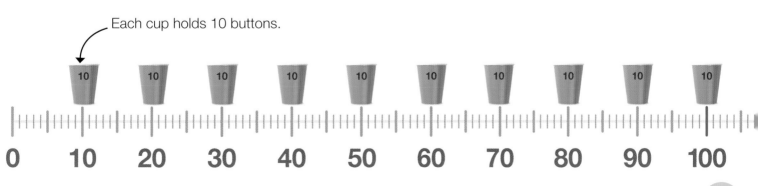

Each cup holds 10 buttons.

0   10   20   30   40   50   60   70   80   90   100

31

Groups of 100

Look around you. Groups of 100 are everywhere. Many of the ways we measure things, such as height, money, weight, and time, are based on groups of 100.

Height charts

A meter (m) is made up of 100 centimeters (cm). We can measure how tall people, animals, and buildings are in meters, or groups of 100 cm.

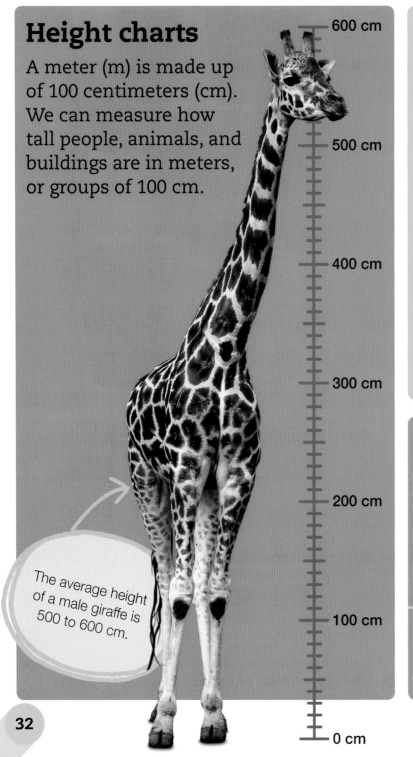

The average height of a male giraffe is 500 to 600 cm.

600 cm

500 cm

400 cm

300 cm

200 cm

100 cm

0 cm

Money

Money is often counted in groups of 100. One dollar ($1) is made up of 100 cents (¢). One pound (£1) is made up of 100 pennies (p). And one euro (€1) is made up of 100 euro cents (c).

Timelines

Important historical dates are often shown on timelines, which usually show years in groups of 100, called centuries.

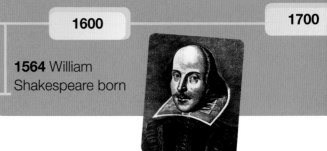

| 1600 | 1700 |

1564 William Shakespeare born

Mass

Cooks use scales—which often show mass in groups of 100 grams—to weigh ingredients for recipes.

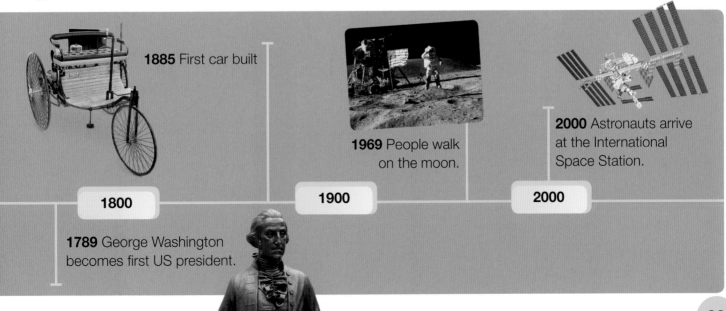

1885 First car built

1969 People walk on the moon.

2000 Astronauts arrive at the International Space Station.

1800

1900

2000

1789 George Washington becomes first US president.

Numbers in 100

The number 100 is made up of **10 equal groups of 10**.
Let's find out how we can split up, or **partition**, 100
into smaller numbers.

Empty 100s chart

This is a 100s chart that doesn't
have any numbers in it. It is a big
square made up of 100 smaller
squares. We can color parts of it
to show numbers inside 100.

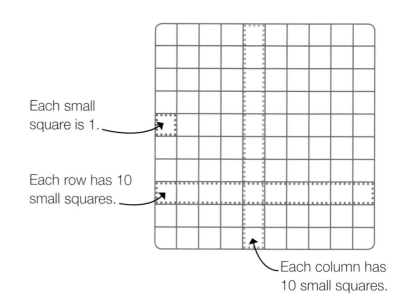

Each small
square is 1.

Each row has 10
small squares.

Each column has
10 small squares.

Partitioning 100

Let's partition 100 to show some of
the smaller numbers inside it, using
a 100s chart and a number line.

This 100s chart has
been partitioned into
2 groups of 50.

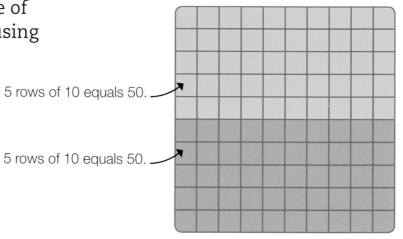

5 rows of 10 equals 50.

5 rows of 10 equals 50.

This number line also shows 100 partitioned into 2 groups of 50.

Each colored bar
equals 50.

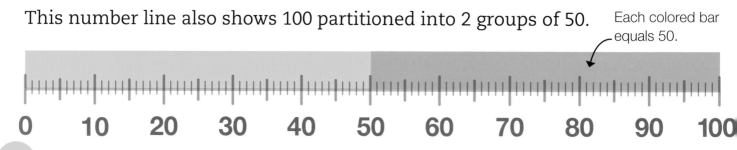

0   10   20   30   40   50   60   70   80   90   100

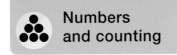

This 100s chart has been partitioned into 5 groups of 20.

2 rows of 10 equals 20.

2 rows of 10 equals 20.

This number line also shows 100 partitioned into 5 groups of 20.

Each colored bar equals 20.

0   10   20   30   40   50   60   70   80   90   100

This 100s chart has been partitioned into a group of 99 small squares and 1 small square.

9 rows of 10 and 9 of the next row equals 99.

The final 1 in the 100s chart.

This number line has been partitioned into 99 and 1.

This long bar equals 99.

This short bar equals 1.

0   10   20   30   40   50   60   70   80   90   100

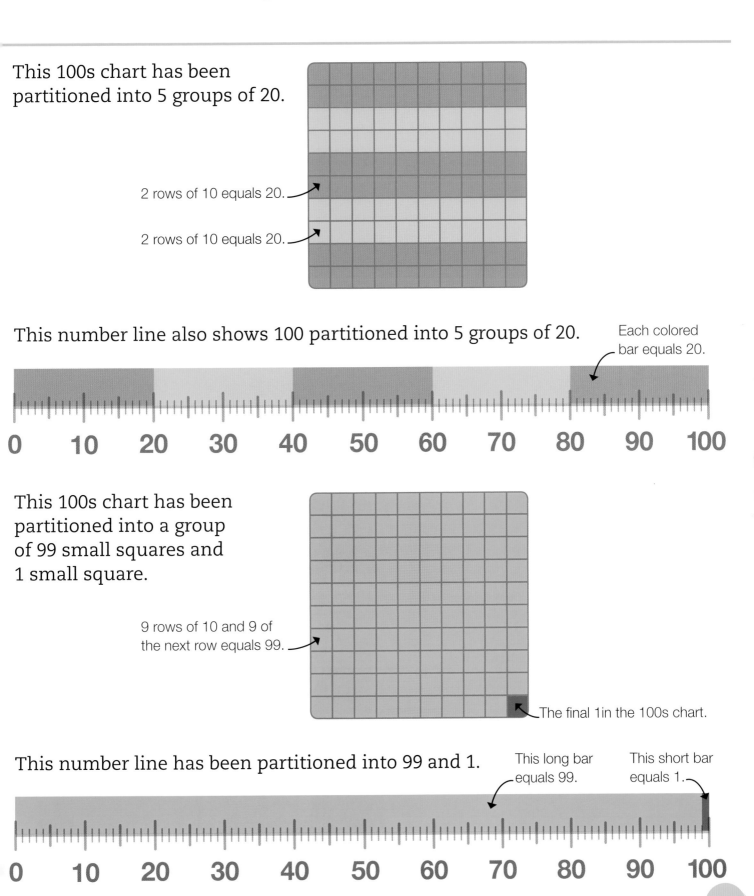

More comparing

To understand how to add, subtract, multiply, and divide, we need to investigate comparisons a little more. We'll use the symbols we learned earlier:

more than **>** less than   less than **<** more than

Bars

Look at these bars. What can we say about their size?

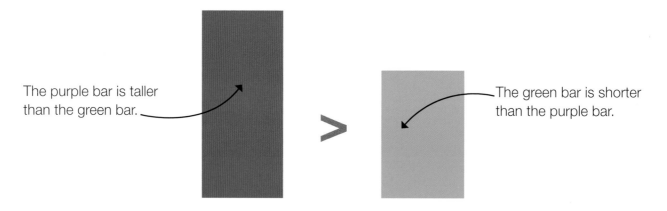

The purple bar is taller than the green bar.

The green bar is shorter than the purple bar.

Now, let's use the bars in a story. Imagine that they stand for 2 drinks. Toby has the purple drink. Tommy has the green drink.

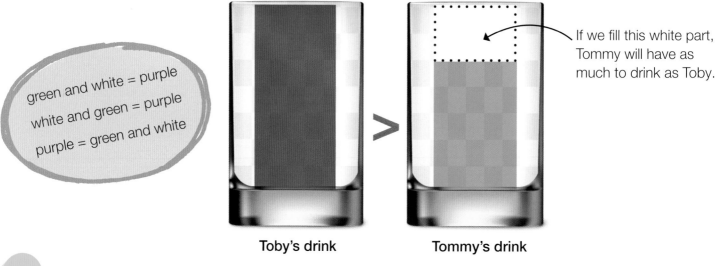

green and white = purple

white and green = purple

purple = green and white

If we fill this white part, Tommy will have as much to drink as Toby.

Toby's drink   Tommy's drink

Let's try another story. Isaac is given some money for his birthday. He spends some of it on a game. We can show this with bars.

This bar stands for all of Isaac's birthday money.

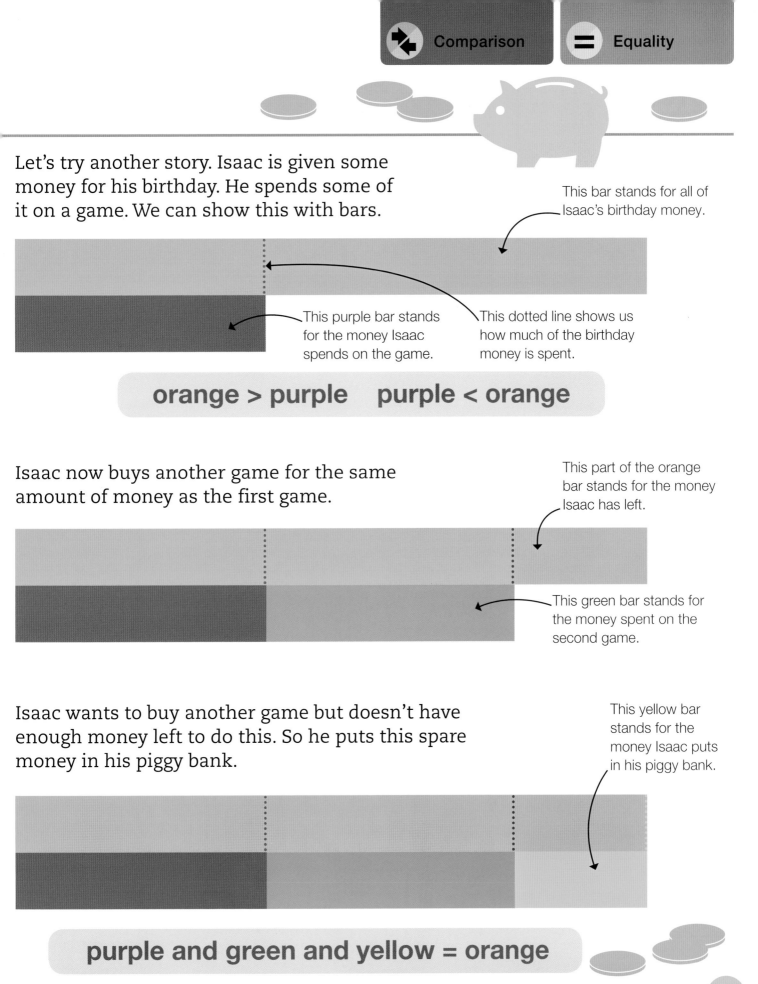

This purple bar stands for the money Isaac spends on the game.

This dotted line shows us how much of the birthday money is spent.

orange > purple   purple < orange

Isaac now buys another game for the same amount of money as the first game.

This part of the orange bar stands for the money Isaac has left.

This green bar stands for the money spent on the second game.

Isaac wants to buy another game but doesn't have enough money left to do this. So he puts this spare money in his piggy bank.

This yellow bar stands for the money Isaac puts in his piggy bank.

purple and green and yellow = orange

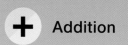

Adding

There are **two different ways** that we can add things. They are known as **joining** and **increasing**. We use the symbol "**+**" to mean **added to**, or **plus**.

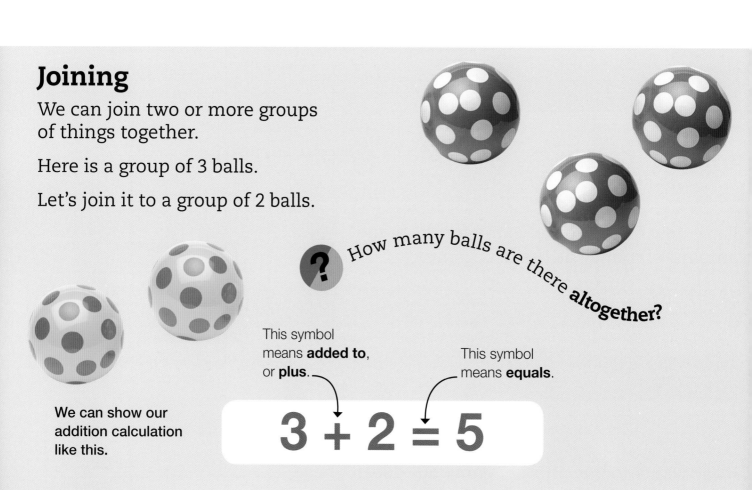

Joining

We can join two or more groups of things together.

Here is a group of 3 balls.

Let's join it to a group of 2 balls.

? How many balls are there altogether?

This symbol means **added to**, or **plus**.

This symbol means **equals**.

We can show our addition calculation like this.

$$3 + 2 = 5$$

Increasing

We can make an amount greater or increase the size of something.

I added more water to my glass, so now I have **more** water in my glass.

Subtracting

There are **two different ways** that we can subtract things. They are known as **partitioning** and **decreasing**. We use the symbol "–" when **subtracting** to mean **take away**, or **minus**.

Partitioning

We can take away a part or parts of a group. This is also known as partitioning.

Here are 5 balls. If we take away 2 of them, we'll only have 3.

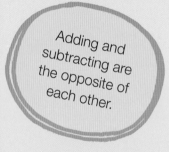
Adding and subtracting are the opposite of each other.

This symbol means **take away**, or **minus**.

This symbol means **equals**.

We can show our subtraction calculation like this.

$$5 - 2 = 3$$

Decreasing

We can make an amount smaller than it was before. This is known as decreasing.

I have drunk some of my water, so now I have **less** water.

Counting on...

Instead of counting everything, another way to add is by **counting on**. Here, we start at the first number in the calculation and then count forward the number of places we are being asked to add.

Counting all the elephants

Imagine we have a group of 6 elephants and a group of 3 elephants, and we want to know the total. We could count each one to do this.

The last number we say tells us the total number of elephants.

$$6 + 3 = 9$$

Counting on from 6

To save time, we can start at 6 and then count on 3 more places to 9.

Sometimes we can move the things we are counting. Placing them in a line helps us count correctly.

6 elephants and then 7, 8, 9 elephants!

... and counting back

If we want to subtract, we can start at the first number in the calculation and then **count back** the number of places we are being asked to subtract.

How many zebras are left?

Here are 9 zebras on the plain. Soon, 3 will leave to visit a watering hole. How many zebras will be left on the plain?

$$9 - 3 = 6$$

Counting back from 9

To make our calculation easier, we are going to arrange our zebras in a line and count back 3 places from 9.

9 zebras minus 3 zebras equals 6 zebras.

41

Adding with ten frames

We've seen that we can add by counting on (see page 40). Now we're going to learn to add using **ten-frame patterns**.

How many balls?

There are 3 balls in a gym bag. We need 2 more balls for our game.

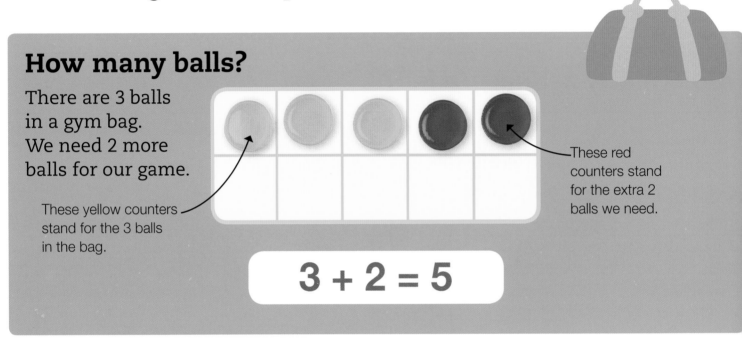

These yellow counters stand for the 3 balls in the bag.

These red counters stand for the extra 2 balls we need.

3 + 2 = 5

How many children?

There are 9 children in a classroom. Then 6 more children arrive. How many children are now in the classroom?

The red counters stand for the 9 children already in the classroom.

The yellow counters stand for the 6 children who enter the classroom.

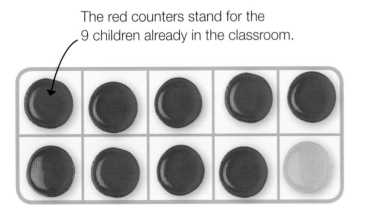

9 + 6 = 15

Subtracting with ten frames

We've seen that we can subtract by counting back (see page 41). Now we're going to learn another way to subtract using **ten-frame patterns**.

How many balls?

There are 10 balls in a gym bag. We need to take out 4 for our game.

These red counters stand for the 6 balls that are left in the bag.

These yellow counters stand for the 4 balls that are taken out of the bag.

$$10 - 4 = 6$$

How many children?

There are 13 children in a classroom. Then 5 children go outside. How many children are now left in the classroom?

These counters stand for the 8 children who stay in the classroom.

The crossed-out counters stand for the 5 children who leave the classroom.

$$13 - 5 = 8$$

Adding on a number line

We can look at **groups of 10** on number lines. Number lines can be easier to use than ten frames when working with bigger numbers.

Using a number line

Let's show the calculation from the bottom of page 42 again, this time using a number line with colored bars. There are 9 children in a classroom, and 6 more arrive.

9 + 6 = 15   9 + 1 = 10 and then **10 + 5 = 15**

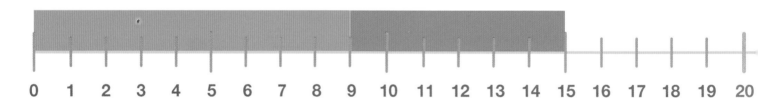

0 1 2 3 4 5 6 7 8 9 10 11 12 13 14 15 16 17 18 19 20

Now let's show a calculation with bigger numbers using a number line.

57 + 6 = 63

57 + 3 = 60 and then **60 + 3 = 63**

Notice we are **partitioning**, or splitting up, the number we are adding. First we complete a **group of 10**. Then we add what's **left over**.

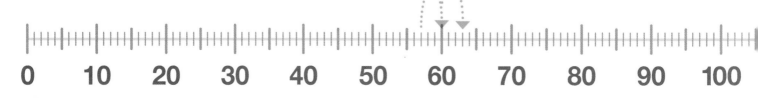

0 10 20 30 40 50 60 70 80 90 100

Subtracting on a number line

Subtraction is the **opposite** of **addition**. **Adding** numbers makes them bigger. **Subtracting** from a number makes it smaller by removing part of it.

Using a number line

Imagine there are 15 children in a classroom, and then 6 of them go outside. Let's show this **subtraction** on a number line. We can partition the number we're subtracting to make the calculation easier.

$$15 - 6 = 9$$ $$15 - 5 = 10$$ and then $$10 - 1 = 9$$

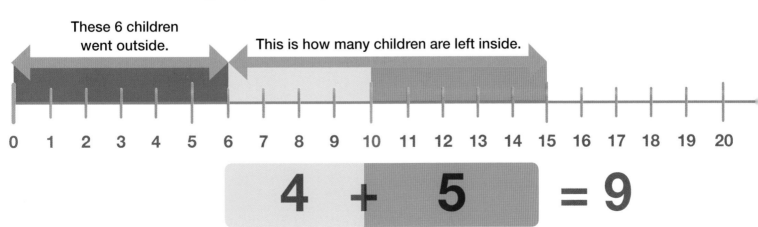

Counting up

We could also solve the calculation above by **counting up** from 6, which is the number we're subtracting, to 15, which is the original number of children. Again, we can pause at 10 to make it easier.

These 6 children went outside.

This is how many children are left inside.

$$4 + 5 = 9$$

Difference

Difference is about looking at amounts that are not equal. It's similar to **comparing** things (see pages 28–29).

Difference in heights

Let's use bars to stand for the heights of the horse and the pony, so we can see the difference between them. When something **isn't equal**, it will be **more** or **less** than something else.

This horse is taller than the pony.

This pony is shorter than the horse.

This bar stands for the height of the horse.

This bar stands for the height of the pony.

The symbol's open side faces the taller animal.

Difference in lengths

We can also use bars to show the difference in lengths, or distances, that a kangaroo and a rabbit can jump.

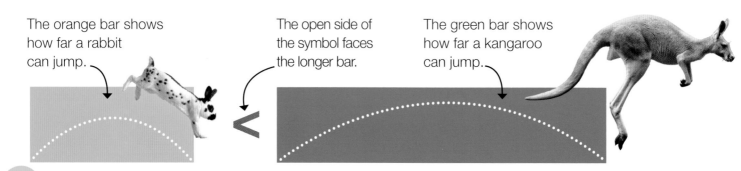

The orange bar shows how far a rabbit can jump.

The open side of the symbol faces the longer bar.

The green bar shows how far a kangaroo can jump.

This shows the difference in the heights of the horse and the pony.

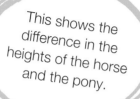

?

If we place the bars next to each other, we can easily see the difference in heights.

Difference using numbers

You can also find difference using numbers.

Here are 7 bananas.

Here are 4 bananas.

Comparing the two patterns, we can see that they are not equal. 7 is more than 4.

The yellow bar stands for the group of 7 bananas.

7 bananas

If we place the bars on top of each other, we can easily see the difference in lengths.

This shows the difference in how far the kangaroo and rabbit can jump.

?

4 bananas

3 bananas

The green bar stands for the group of 4 bananas.

The **difference is 3.**

We could also write this as

7 – 4 = 3

Difference on a number line

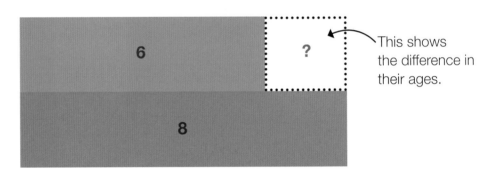

When we compare two different amounts that we can **measure** in the same way, the **difference** between them can be found using a number line.

Using a bar model

Abemelek is 6 and his sister Yohanna is 8 years old. What's the difference in their ages? First, let's show it using a bar model.

6	?

This shows the difference in their ages.

8

We can use a number line to find the difference in the bars.

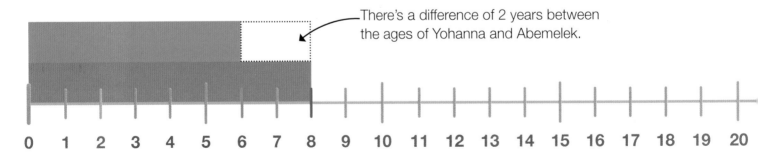

There's a difference of 2 years between the ages of Yohanna and Abemelek.

0 1 2 3 4 5 6 7 8 9 10 11 12 13 14 15 16 17 18 19 20

This difference can also be written using just numbers:

$$8 - 6 = 2$$

Using ten frames

Ten frames can also be used to show difference, such as between the prices of two ice-cream cones at a school fair.

41¢

35¢

Here, the price of each ice-cream cone is shown on ten frames.

41

35

We can also use a number line to find the difference that we can see on the ten frames.

There's a difference of 6¢ between the prices of the ice-cream cones.

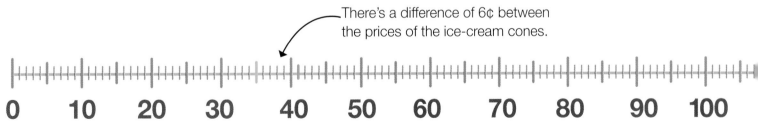

0   10   20   30   40   50   60   70   80   90   100

This difference can also be written using just numbers:

$$41 - 35 = 6$$

Multiplying

Multiplying is a way of adding together lots of the same number, which is called **repeated addition**, or of increasing the size of something by the same amount lots of times, which is called **scaling**. We use the symbol "**×**" to mean **multiplied by**, or **times**.

Repeated addition

Look at these 6 colorful stones. We can see that we have 3 groups of 2 stones, or 2 groups of 3 stones.

$$2 + 2 + 2 = 6$$
3 groups of 2

or

$$3 + 3 = 6$$
2 groups of 3

This can be written as

$$2 \times 3 = 6$$

$$3 \times 2 = 6$$

This symbol means **multiplied by** or **times**.

Scaling

Look at these buildings. The second building is two-times (× 2) taller than the first building. The third building is two-times (× 2) taller than the second building.

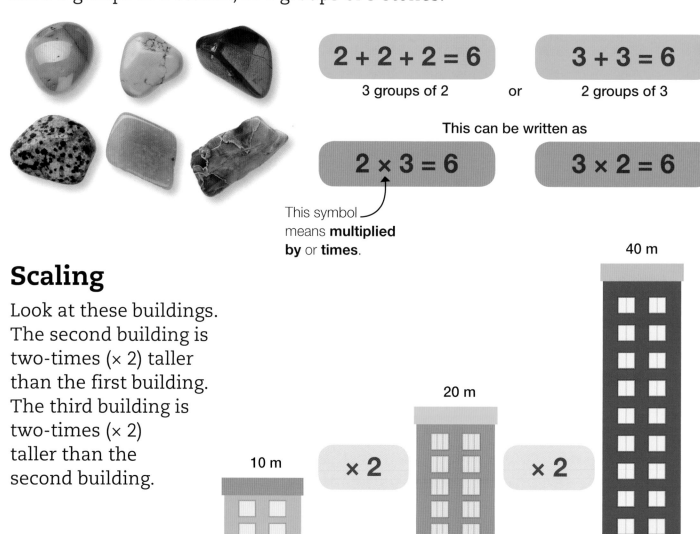

40 m

20 m

10 m

× 2

× 2

Dividing

Dividing is splitting up an amount into smaller, equal amounts. If you know how big you want the smaller amounts to be, it is called **grouping**. If you know how many smaller groups you want, it is called **sharing**. We use the symbol "÷" to mean **divided by**.

Grouping

If you have 9 stones and decide to split them into groups of 4, you will have 2 groups of 4, and 1 stone left over, which is called a **remainder** (r).

This symbol means **divided by**.

$$9 \div 4 = 2 \text{ r } 1$$

Sharing

If you have 10 shells and you want to split them into 2 equal groups, you will have 5 shells in each group.

$$10 \div 2 = 5$$

Multiplying with arrays

A helpful way to learn to multiply is to look at **arrays**. They let us make calculations using **repeated addition** (see page 50).

Arrays

Eggs are often packed in boxes made up of **rows and columns**. In math, this pattern is called an **array**.

$$3 \times 2 = 2 \times 3$$

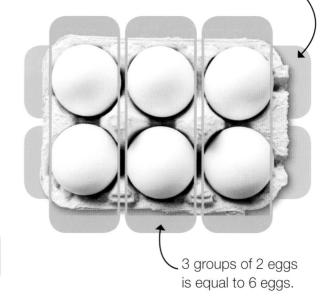

2 groups of 3 eggs is equal to 6 eggs.

3 groups of 2 eggs is equal to 6 eggs.

? Can you see that 2 × 3 and 3 × 2 are both equal to 6?

Here you may see 3 groups of 4 balloons, or 4 groups of 3.

$$3 \times 4 = 4 \times 3$$

Look again. You may also see 6 groups of 2 balloons, or 2 groups of 6 balloons.

$$6 \times 2 = 2 \times 6$$

Dividing with arrays

We can also use **arrays** to split up amounts. Arrays help us divide using **grouping** or **sharing** (see page 51).

Arrays

Let's look at how we can divide up an array of 6 eggs.

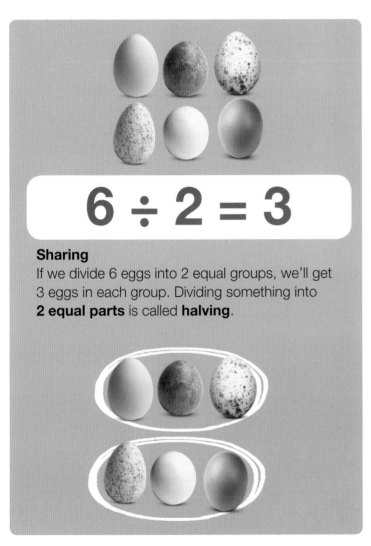

6 ÷ 2 = 3

Sharing
If we divide 6 eggs into 2 equal groups, we'll get 3 eggs in each group. Dividing something into **2 equal parts** is called **halving**.

6 ÷ 3 = 2

Grouping
If we divide 6 eggs into equal groups of 2, we'll get 3 groups of 2 eggs.

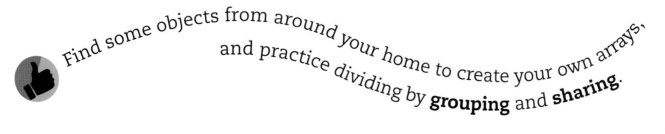

Find some objects from around your home to create your own arrays, and practice dividing by **grouping** and **sharing**.

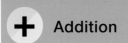 
Multiplying with ten frames

We can use ten frames to **multiply** numbers. Remember that multiplication can be seen as **repeated addition** (see page 50), in which we add an equal amount over and over again.

Groups of 4

Let's multiply groups of 4. We start with 2 groups of 2. Each time we fill the ten frame, we add 2 more groups of 2.

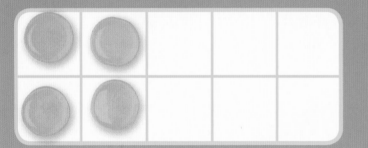

Can you see that 2 groups of 2 is the same as 1 group of 4?

$4 \times 1 = 4$

This is the same as 1 group of 4.

$4 \times 2 = 8$

This is the same as 2 groups of 4.

$4 \times 3 = 12$

This is the same as 3 groups of 4.

Dividing with ten frames

Using ten frames is also a good way to **divide up** an amount into smaller, equal amounts by using **grouping** (see page 51).

Equal grouping

This way of dividing means that we split the total amount into equally sized groups. Sometimes there will be a **remainder** (see page 51).

Let's divide 24 counters into equal groups of 4.
First, we can arrange the 24 counters in ten frames.

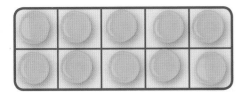
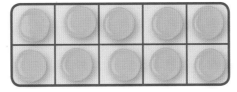
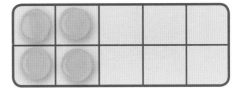

Then we can show equal groups of 4 counters along the ten frames by putting different colored boxes behind each group. Now it's easy to see how many groups of 4 there are in 24.

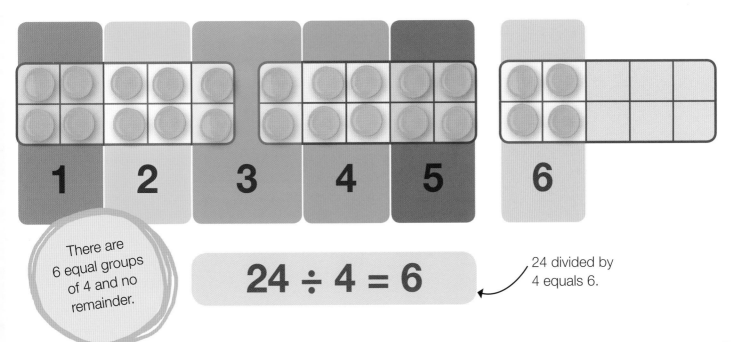

There are 6 equal groups of 4 and no remainder.

$$24 \div 4 = 6$$

24 divided by 4 equals 6.

Multiplying on a number line

Using a number line to multiply can be **quicker and easier** than using ten frames.

Groups of 4

There are 4 children in a group. Let's use a number line to figure out how many children there would be altogether if there were 6 of these groups of 4.

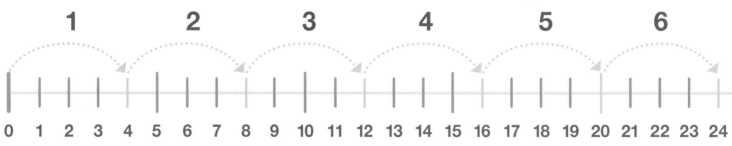

$$4 \times 6 = 24$$

6 groups of 4 children make 24.

What's the order?

It doesn't matter what order you multiply numbers in. 6 × 4 equals 24 and so does 4 × 6.

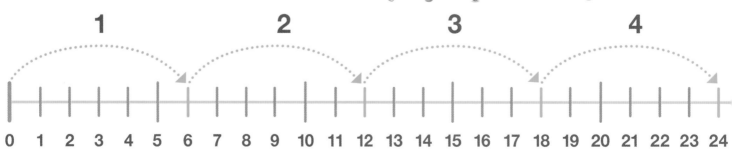

$$6 \times 4 = 24$$

4 groups of 6 children make 24.

Dividing on a number line

Using a number line to divide can be **quicker and easier** than using ten frames.

Multiplication and division are **opposites**!

Equal grouping

Let's now use a number line to divide the 24 children into equal groups of 4.

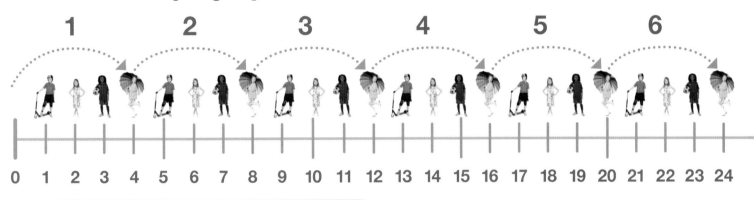

$$24 \div 4 = 6$$

There are 6 equal groups of 4 in 24.

How many?

Now let's use a number line to find out how many desserts you can make with 26 strawberries, if you need 5 strawberries for each dessert.

1 strawberry remains.

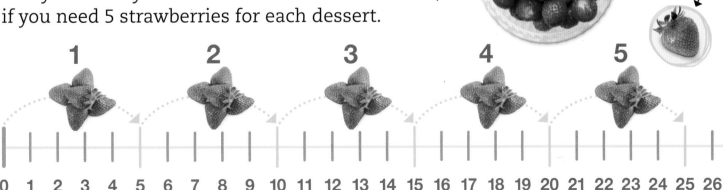

$$26 \div 5 = 5 \text{ r } 1$$

There are 5 groups of 5 strawberries with a remainder (r) of 1.

Odd and even

When a whole number can be **divided by 2** without leaving a remainder, it is an **even** number. All other numbers are **odd**.

Using an array

Let's arrange 8 dogs in an array to see if the number 8 is odd or even. We can see from the array that 8 can be divided into 2 groups of 4 without a remainder, so **8 is even**. We can also see that 8 is made up of 4 groups of 2. All even numbers are made up of groups of 2.

The last digits of even numbers follow this pattern:
0 2 4 6 8

The last digits of odd numbers follow this pattern:
1 3 5 7 9

Woof!

$$8 \div 2 = 4$$ and $$8 \div 4 = 2$$

Adding odd and even numbers

When you add two numbers together, there are rules about whether the answer is odd or even. Let's use ten frames to show how these rules work.

even + even

 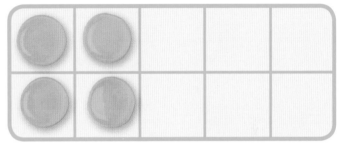

8 + 6 = 14   So, even + even = even

even + odd

8 + 5 = 13   So, even + odd = odd

odd + odd

9 + 7 = 16   So, odd + odd = even

59

Building times tables

Times tables show the numbers we get when we **multiply** a number by 1, then 2, then 3, and so on. They are often called **multiplication tables**. We can use ten frames, number lines, and even our fingers to help us learn these tables.

Ten-frame patterns

Ten-frame patterns can help us build the **2 times table**. As you add pairs of pineapples, you see how the table builds up.

2 × 1 = 2   2 × 2 = 4   2 × 3 = 6   2 × 4 = 8   2 × 5 = 10

Number line

We also can use a number line to see the answers in times tables. Here are the answers to the first 6 steps in the **2 times table**.

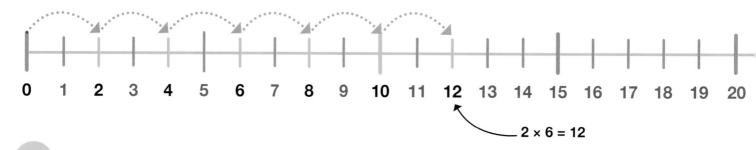

2 × 6 = 12

Fingers and thumbs

We can use fingers and thumbs to show steps in the **5 times table**.

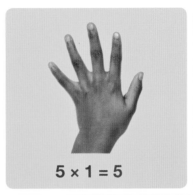
5 × 1 = 5

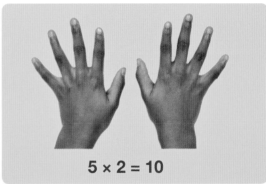
5 × 2 = 10

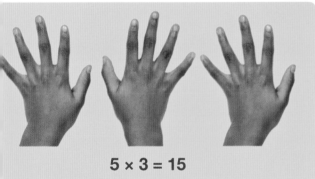
5 × 3 = 15

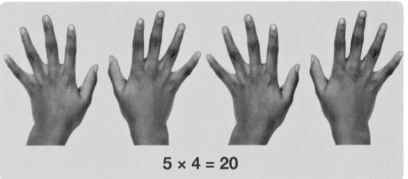
5 × 4 = 20

👍 You can practice the **4 times table** if you don't use your thumbs.

Ten frames

We can use ten frames filled with counters to show the **10 times table**.

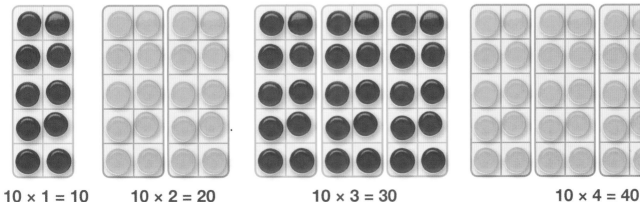
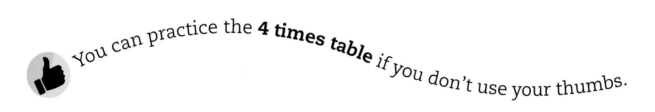

10 × 1 = 10   10 × 2 = 20   10 × 3 = 30   10 × 4 = 40

61

Times tables

We looked at ways to build times tables on pages 60–61. Here are 3 tables you'll find very useful. They are the 2, 5, and 10 times tables.

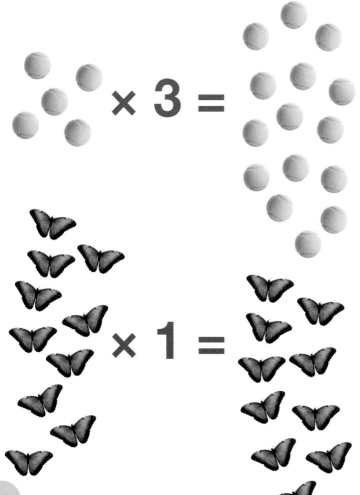

2 times table

For 2 times a number, you double the number.

$$2 \times 1 = 2$$
$$2 \times 2 = 4$$
$$2 \times 3 = 6$$
$$2 \times 4 = 8$$
$$2 \times 5 = 10$$
$$2 \times 6 = 12$$
$$2 \times 7 = 14$$
$$2 \times 8 = 16$$
$$2 \times 9 = 18$$
$$2 \times 10 = 20$$
$$2 \times 11 = 22$$
$$2 \times 12 = 24$$

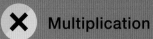 

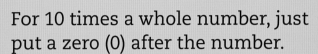

5 times table

Use your fingers to help you with the 5 times table (see page 61).

5 × 1 = 5

5 × 2 = 10

5 × 3 = 15

5 × 4 = 20

5 × 5 = 25

5 × 6 = 30

5 × 7 = 35

5 × 8 = 40

5 × 9 = 45

5 × 10 = 50

5 × 11 = 55

5 × 12 = 60

10 times table

For 10 times a whole number, just put a zero (0) after the number.

10 × 1 = 10

10 × 2 = 20

10 × 3 = 30

10 × 4 = 40

10 × 5 = 50

10 × 6 = 60

10 × 7 = 70

10 × 8 = 80

10 × 9 = 90

10 × 10 = 100

10 × 11 = 110

10 × 12 = 120

Multiples

The numbers you get when you do times tables are sometimes called **multiples**. We can also show multiples in **arrays**, on **number lines**, and in **100s charts**.

Arrays

Arrays (see page 21) can help us figure out multiples in times tables. Look at how this array of cupcakes can help you with the **4 times table**.

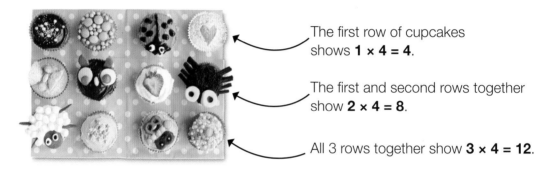

The first row of cupcakes shows **1 × 4 = 4**.

The first and second rows together show **2 × 4 = 8**.

All 3 rows together show **3 × 4 = 12**.

Number lines

It doesn't matter which number we write first when we multiply 2 numbers together—you will always get the same multiple. We can show this on number lines. First, we can see that 5 groups of 3 equals 15.

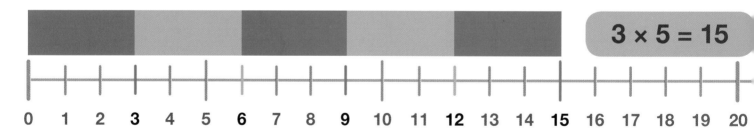

$$3 \times 5 = 15$$

0 1 2 3 4 5 6 7 8 9 10 11 12 13 14 15 16 17 18 19 20

Now, we can see that 3 groups of 5 also equals 15.

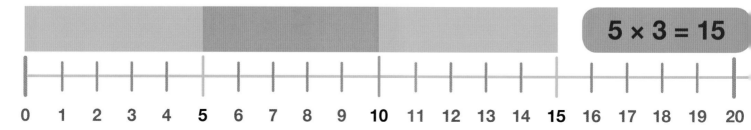

$$5 \times 3 = 15$$

0 1 2 3 4 5 6 7 8 9 10 11 12 13 14 15 16 17 18 19 20

100s chart

We can show multiples on a 100s chart. Below, multiples of 3 and 5 are highlighted. You can also see multiples shared by both 3 and 5 (called common multiples), such as 15 and 30.

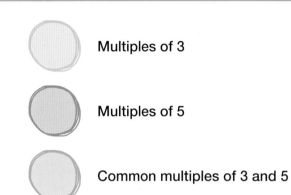

○ Multiples of 3

○ Multiples of 5

○ Common multiples of 3 and 5

21 is a multiple of 3.
7 × 3 = 21

10 is a multiple of 5.
2 × 5 = 10

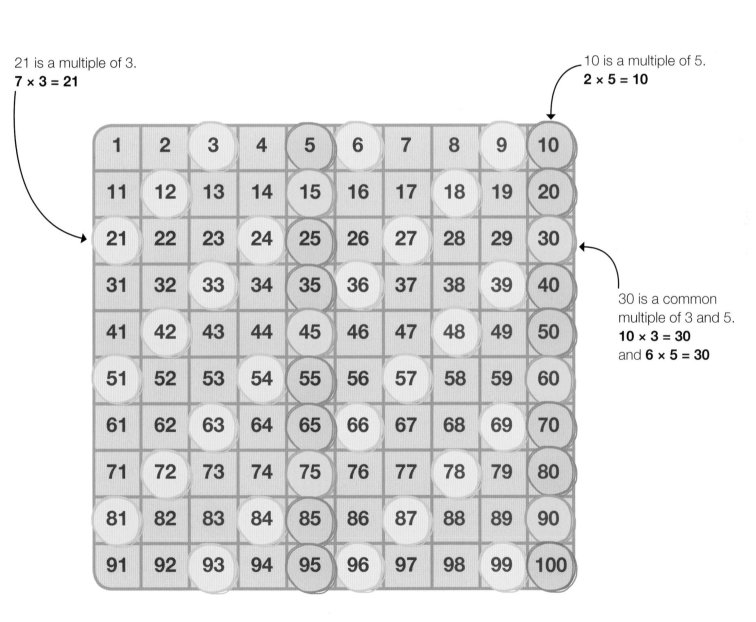

30 is a common multiple of 3 and 5.
10 × 3 = 30
and **6 × 5 = 30**

Multiplying by 10

When we multiply something by 10, we get 10 times that amount. We can use **ten-frame patterns** to show how it works.

2 times 10

We have 2 mugs, which is the same as 2 mugs × 1. But we want 10 times that number of mugs, so let's show what 2 mugs × 10 will look like.

2 mugs × 1 = 2

If we arrange the mugs in ten-frame patterns, we can see that 10 groups of 2 mugs fills 2 ten frames exactly.

1 group of 2 mugs

5 groups of 2 mugs = 10 mugs

5 groups of 2 mugs = 10 mugs

10 mugs + 10 mugs = 20 mugs

This is the same as

2 mugs × 10 = 20 mugs

Note that when you multiply a whole number by 10, you put a 0 next to it. So **2** becomes **20**.

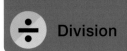
5 times 10

Let's see how we can use ten-frame patterns to multiply other numbers by 10. This time, we'll try 5 counters × 10.

$5 \times 1 = 5$

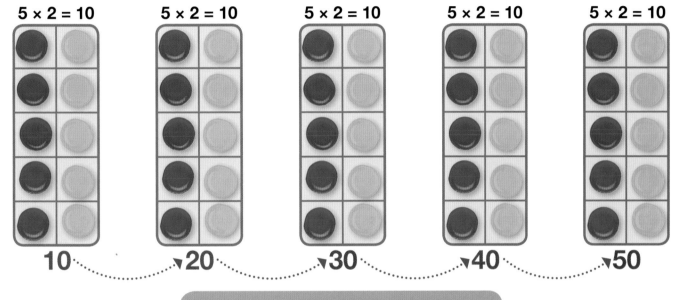

$5 \times 2 = 10$ $5 \times 2 = 10$ $5 \times 2 = 10$ $5 \times 2 = 10$ $5 \times 2 = 10$

10 ⟶ 20 ⟶ 30 ⟶ 40 ⟶ 50

$$5 \times 10 = 50$$

3 times 10

Now let's try multiplying 3 by 10.

$3 \times 1 = 3$

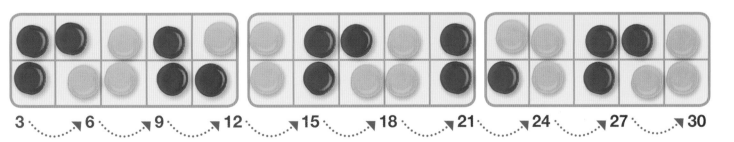

3 ⟶ 6 ⟶ 9 ⟶ 12 ⟶ 15 ⟶ 18 ⟶ 21 ⟶ 24 ⟶ 27 ⟶ 30

$$3 \times 10 = 30$$

Fractions

A fraction is **part of a whole** thing or group of things. They're everywhere in real life—an amount of fruit can be split into fractions, for example. Seeing how we use fractions in our lives helps us understand them.

Dividing equally

Fractions are made when something is divided into smaller parts or groups. The simplest way to divide something is to split it into equal parts. For example, a group of 8 raspberries can be divided equally in three ways—into groups of 1, 2, or 4.

8 raspberries

8 divided into 8 equal parts (groups) makes 1 in each part.

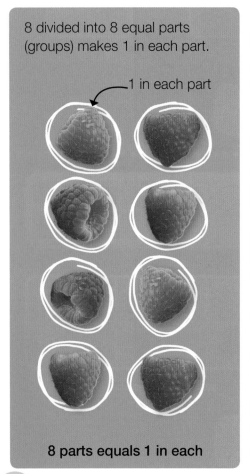

1 in each part

8 parts equals 1 in each

8 divided into 4 equal parts (groups) makes 2 in each part.

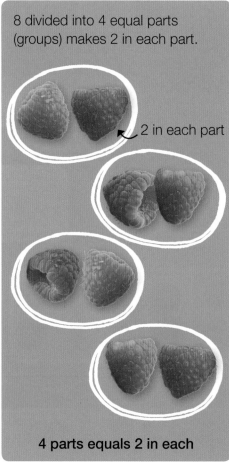

2 in each part

4 parts equals 2 in each

8 divided into 2 equal parts (groups) makes 4 in each part.

4 in each part

2 parts equals 4 in each

Two equal parts

There are different ways to divide something into two equal parts, or halves. One way would be to say *"One for you, one for me..."* until none are left. The number of items or pieces in each group or part can then be counted.

Ten frames

Ten frames can also be used to divide a number into two equal parts. When the grapes are arranged in the frames, you can see how many there are in each part.

14 grapes are split equally into 2 parts on these ten frames.

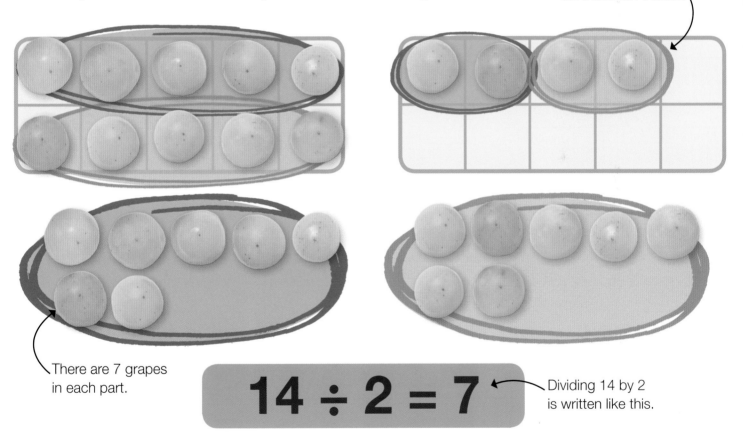

There are 7 grapes in each part.

14 ÷ 2 = 7

Dividing 14 by 2 is written like this.

The whole amount has been divided into 2 equal parts, called **fractions.**

Each of the 2 parts is called a **half**, which we write like this (see also page 71):

½

Halves and quarters

A fraction is 1 or more **equal parts of a whole**.
A **half (½)** is 1 of 2 equal parts of a whole.
A **quarter (¼)** is 1 of 4 equal parts of a whole.

Dividing up

This pizza has been divided into 2 equal parts to make
2 halves and into 4 equal parts to make 4 quarters.

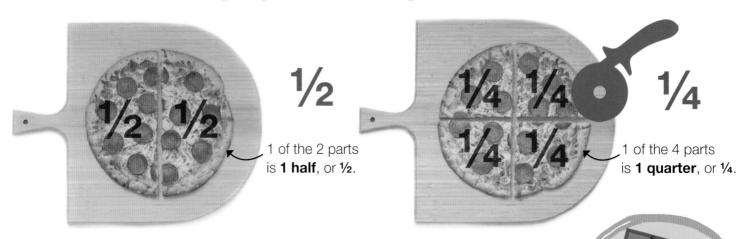

½

1 of the 2 parts
is **1 half**, or ½.

¼

1 of the 4 parts
is **1 quarter**, or ¼.

Chocolate fractions

A bar of chocolate can also be divided into halves
and quarters. Let's look at how this is done.

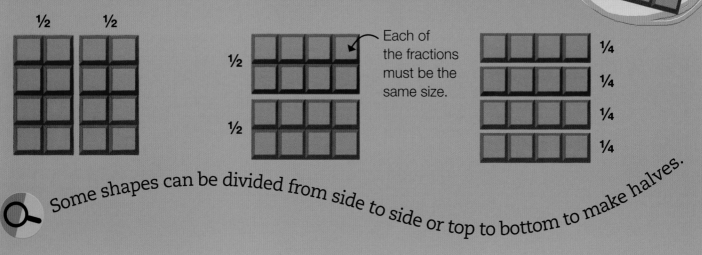

½   ½

½

½

Each of
the fractions
must be the
same size.

¼

¼

¼

¼

🔍 Some shapes can be divided from side to side or top to bottom to make halves.

70

Writing fractions

Did you notice that fractions are written using 2 numbers separated by a line? For example, 1 quarter, which is 1 of 4 equal parts, is written as ¼.

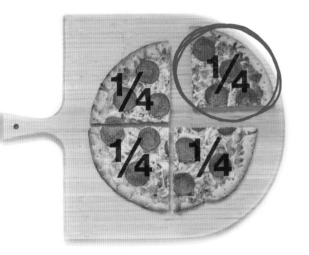

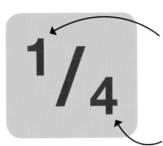

1 shows the number of equal parts in the fraction.

4 shows the number of equal parts that the whole amount has been divided into.

If 2 quarters of the pizza are eaten, we have 2 quarters of the whole pizza left.

2 shows the number of equal parts that remain of the pizza.

4 shows the number of equal parts that the whole pizza has been divided into.

Q **2 quarters** are equal to **1 half**.

$$\frac{2}{4} = \frac{1}{2}$$

71

Adding halves

Fractions can be added together to make bigger fractions and sometimes whole numbers. Let's add some halves.

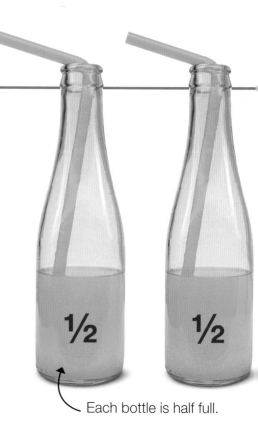

Each bottle is half full.

Adding 2 halves

We see halves of things all around us. For example, if we buy a bottle of juice and drink half of it, we will have half a bottle left. When another half bottle of juice is added to the first one, we have enough juice to fill a whole bottle.

½	½

=

1 whole

We can use colored bars to show that 2 half bottles of juice make a whole bottle of juice.

Adding three halves

2 half bottles of juice added together make 1 whole bottle of juice. If another half bottle is added, this makes 1 whole and 1 half bottle of juice. Here is another way of writing this:

$$½ + ½ + ½ = 1½$$

Adding lots of halves

If 2 halves make 1 whole, then adding another 2 halves will make a total of 2 wholes. An easy way to add lots of halves together is to first put any sets of 2 halves together to make wholes.

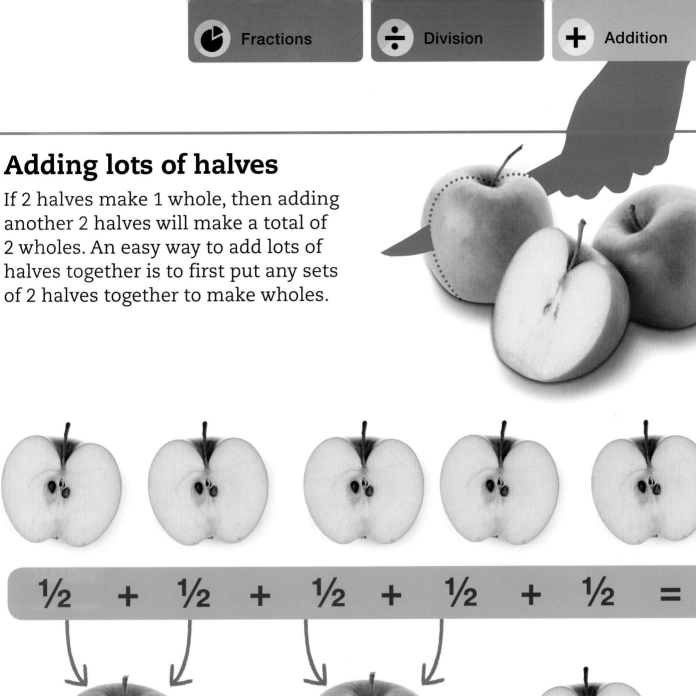

½ + ½ + ½ + ½ + ½ =

1 whole   1 whole   1 half

1 + 1 + ½ =

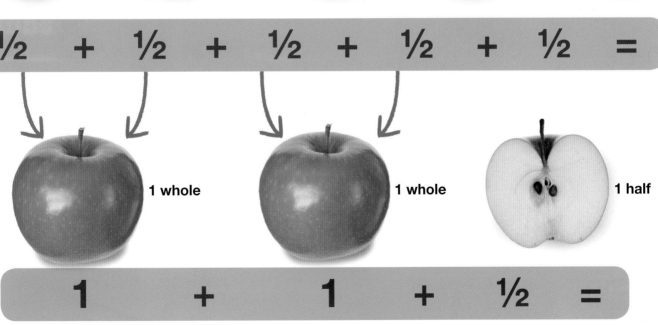

2 ½

Adding 5 halves together makes 2 wholes and 1 half.

73

Measuring

We **measure** things to find their **exact size**, such as how high, or how long, or how heavy they are. We also measure time, how hot or cold things are, how fast things move, how old we are, and how much money we have.

What can we measure?

Here are some of the things that you can measure.

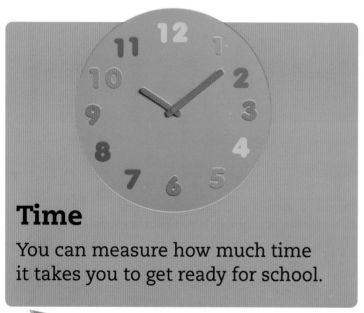

Time

You can measure how much time it takes you to get ready for school.

Ingredients

You can measure the ingredients you'll need to bake a cake.

Money

You can measure, or figure out, if you have enough money to buy a toy or an ice-cream cone.

Length

You can measure how far you or your friends, or a frog or another animal, can leap.

Speed

You can look at the speedometer inside a car to measure how fast or slow the car is going.

Age

You can measure your age by figuring out how old you are in years and months.

Temperature

You can measure the temperature of a room to see how hot or cold it is at different times of day.

The tallest trees are more than 50 times the height of a fully grown person.

Height

You can measure the height of something to find out how tall it is. Try measuring your own height, or the height of a plant or some flowers.

Frogs can leap 20 times the length of their own bodies.

Standard measurements

To measure things accurately, we use what we call **units of measurement** that are a **fixed** size. These are called **standard units** and are the same all over the world.

Fixed measurements

Standard units help us share information about the size of things with other people, because standard units are exactly the same size everywhere. Here are some of the most common standard units that we use.

To measure **length**, **distance**, and **height**, you can use these units:

inches (in)
feet (ft)
yards (yd)
miles (mi)
millimeters (mm)
centimeters (cm)
meters (m)
kilometers (km)

To measure **mass**, you can use these units:

ounces (oz)
pounds (lb)
tons (tn)
milligrams (mg)
grams (g)
kilograms (kg)

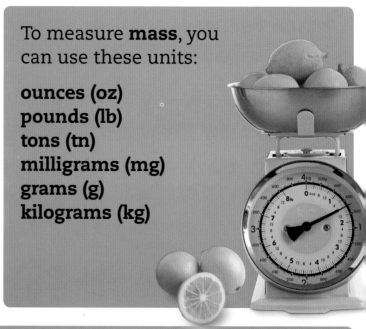

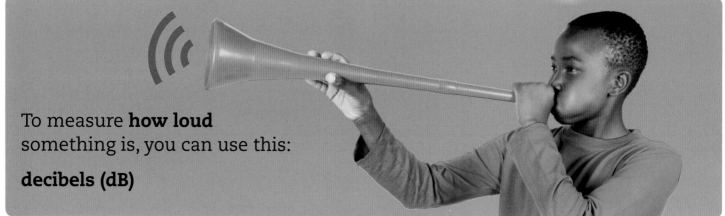

To measure **how loud** something is, you can use this:

decibels (dB)

To measure **temperature**, or how hot or cold something is, you can use these units:

degrees Fahrenheit (°F)
degrees Celsius (°C)

These units are named after the scientists **Daniel Fahrenheit** and **Anders Celsius.**

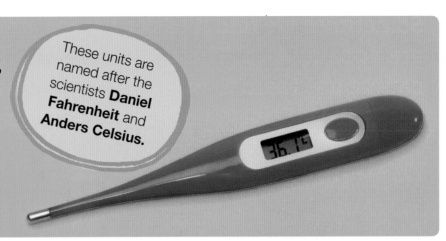

To measure **capacity**, or how much a container can hold, you can use these units:

fluid ounces (fl oz)
pints (pt)
quarts (qt)
liters (l)
gallons (gal)

To measure **time**, you use these:

seconds (sec)
minutes (min)
hours (h)
days
weeks
months
years

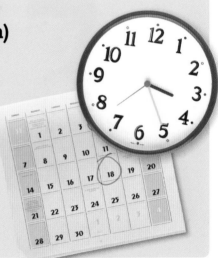

To measure the **speed** that something is moving at, such as a car, van, or even the wind, you can use these units:

feet per second (ft/sec)
miles per hour (mph)
meters per second (m/s)
kilometers per hour (kmh)

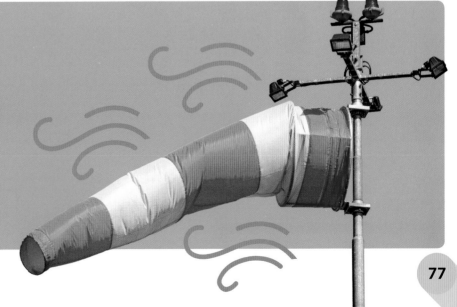

Nonstandard measurements

Sometimes we find it easier to measure things in units that are **nonstandard**. These units are not fixed in size, so you cannot use them to measure something accurately, but they can give you a very good idea of how big something is.

Human units

You can use parts of your body to measure the size of things.

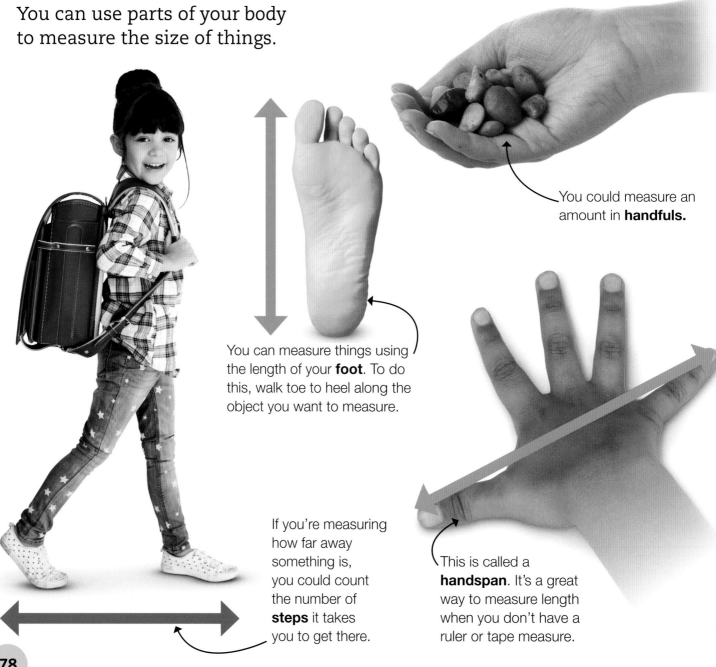

You could measure an amount in **handfuls.**

You can measure things using the length of your **foot**. To do this, walk toe to heel along the object you want to measure.

If you're measuring how far away something is, you could count the number of **steps** it takes you to get there.

This is called a **handspan**. It's a great way to measure length when you don't have a ruler or tape measure.

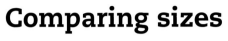
Comparing sizes

It can be easier to understand how big something is when you compare its size to the size of something else.

The Great Pyramid at Giza in Egypt was once the tallest building in the world. But the height of the Empire State Building is equal to 3 Great Pyramids standing on top of each other!

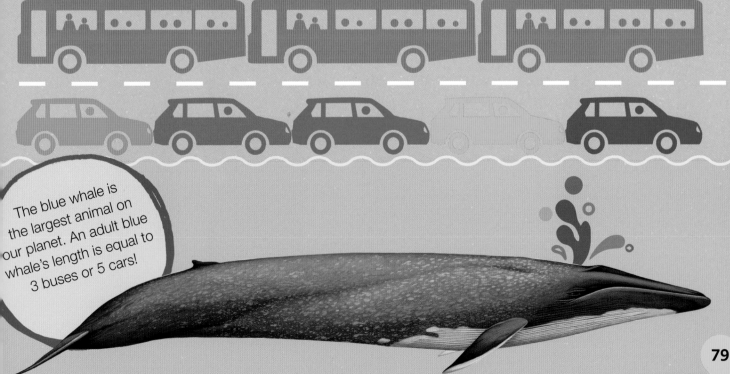

The blue whale is the largest animal on our planet. An adult blue whale's length is equal to 3 buses or 5 cars!

Length, height, and depth

When we measure an object's **length**, we want to know how **long** it is. When we measure its **height**, we want to know how **high** or **tall** it is. When we measure its **depth**, we want to know how **deep** or **wide** it is.

Measuring

There are some important rules to remember when measuring length, height, or depth.

To measure in standard units (see page 76), such as inches or centimeters, you need a measuring tool, such as a ruler or tape measure, with those units on it.

You must line up your ruler or tape measure so that the 0 on its scale is level with the place you are measuring from.

To measure correctly with a tape measure, you must keep it as straight as possible.

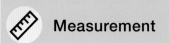
Is it big enough?

You may want to pack
something in a box. It would
be useful to measure the
length, height, and depth
of the box to find out if it
is big enough.

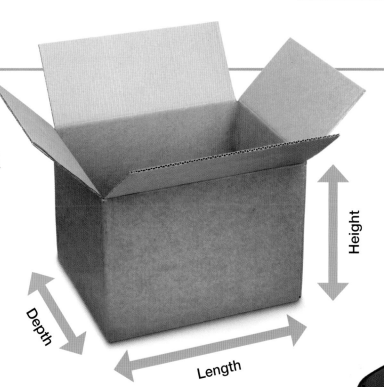

Height

Depth

Length

Units of measurement

You can measure length, height, and depth using **yards (yd)**,
feet (ft), and **inches (in)**, or **meters (m)**, **centimeters (cm)**, and
millimeters (mm).

This tape measure
shows both inches
and centimeters.

1 meter

Both this ruler and this measuring
wheel measure 1 meter in length.
The meter on the wheel is a circular
shape, so you can push it along the
ground to measure longer distances.

1 meter

Mass

We often use the word **weight** instead of **mass**. However, when we weigh something, we are really finding its mass, which is a measure of the amount of matter, or material, in an object.

Units of measurement

We measure mass using units such as **ounces (oz)** and **pounds (lb)**, or **grams (g)** and **kilograms (kg)**. We often see these units used in recipes and on boxes, jars, and cans of food in the supermarket.

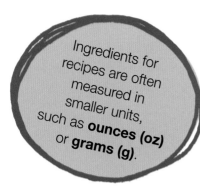

Ingredients for recipes are often measured in smaller units, such as **ounces (oz)** or **grams (g)**.

 We can find out an object's mass using **scales**. Look at the numbers on this kitchen scale. Can you see that they are part of a curved number line?

Larger masses

When we want to measure a person or a really heavy object, we need scales that measure in larger units, such as pounds or kilograms. You might have scales like this in your bathroom.

You stand on these scales to weigh yourself.

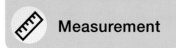

Types of scales

With some scales, the object being weighed presses down and makes a needle move along a number line, showing its mass. With others, you balance what you are weighing against metal pieces of known mass, called weights. There are also scales that measure mass electronically.

The mass of the kitten pushes the red needle down.

Hanging scales are often used in supermarkets.

These electronic scales have a digital readout.

You balance the unknown mass you are weighing against a known metal mass to use these scales.

A person might weigh **168 lb (76 kg)** and an adult elephant **13,200 lb (6,000 kg)**. You'd need very special scales to measure an elephant's mass!

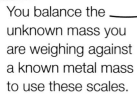

Capacity

When we measure how much **space** there is inside a container, we are measuring its **capacity**. We usually use standard units, such as **pints (pt)**, **fluid ounces (fl oz)**, **liters (l)**, and **milliliters (ml)**, to measure capacity.

Measuring capacity

To find the capacity of a container, first fill it to the top with a liquid. Then pour the liquid into a measuring cup, and read the scale.

This striped jug has a capacity of about 20 fl oz (550 ml).

550 ml

This scale shows fluid ounces (fl oz).

This scale shows milliliters (ml).

Recipes

We often use a measuring cup to measure exactly the right amount of liquid for a recipe.

Measuring spoons

We use **measuring spoons** to measure small amounts of ingredients when we're preparing food. The size of the inside of the spoon is its capacity.

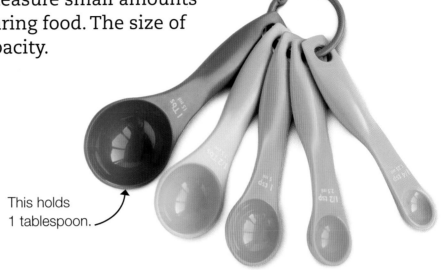

This holds 1 tablespoon.

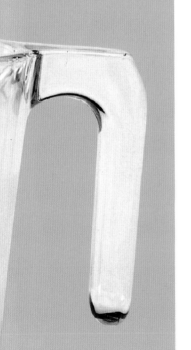

The label on a bottle of juice tells you the **volume** of the juice it contains. But bottles are never filled to the very top, so this volume of liquid is only roughly equal to the **capacity** of the bottle.

Capacity and volume

The **capacity** of the measuring cup on the left is the amount it can hold when filled to the top, which is just over 1 liter. However, if the measuring cup is only filled to half of its capacity, the **volume** of liquid in it is 500 ml.

Estimating

Estimating is having an idea of how many or how much there is of something **without counting or measuring**. It often involves looking for **patterns** in the groups of things you are estimating the number or amount of.

How many?

Let's look at the beads below and **estimate** how many there are. Don't look for too long. Make your estimate quickly, then cover them up.

You could do this several times to help you be more confident about your estimate, but only ever look at the beads for a very short time. How many beads do you think you saw? Which is closest to your **estimate?** Ten, 22, or 28?

The more you practice noticing **patterns** and **groups** of things, the better you'll be at estimating.

Bigger challenge

A bird-watcher will often **estimate** the size of a flock of birds that they can see through their binoculars. Look at the picture below and estimate how many birds there are.

When you've made a few estimates, place something small, such as a bead, on each bird in the picture. Then arrange the beads into **ten-frame patterns**. This way, it's easy to see how many birds there are without actually counting! How good were your estimates?

There are many ways to improve your **estimating skills**. Try estimating how long your bed is in handspans (see page 78). Look carefully at your hand, and imagine it measuring your bed.

My day

We split our day up into different blocks of **time**, such as morning, afternoon, evening, and night. **Measuring** a day in this way helps us organize our lives.

Morning
Get out of bed
Wash face
Eat breakfast

Midday
Lunchtime
Talk to friends

Afternoon
Math lesson
Story time
School day ends

Evening
Eat dinner
Do homework

Night
Set alarm clock
Brush teeth

What time of day?

Time helps us organize our lives by allowing us to put events in order. It lets us know what comes before and after something else, and at what time of day things happen.

Pack schoolbag

Brush teeth

Walk to school

School day begins

Eat lunch

Read a book

Play soccer

Take the school bus home

Swimming lesson

Listen to music

Relax

Have a bubble bath

ZZZzz

Get ready for bed

Hours and minutes

Time, like length and mass, can be measured in **equal fixed units**. There are several different-sized **units of time**, but they are all related to each other.

Hours in a day

We divide each day into 24 equal units, called hours. Then, we usually split these **24 hours** into two groups of 12 hours and use clocks to tell us what hour of the day (or night) it is.

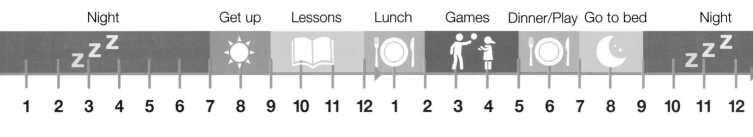

| Night | Get up | Lessons | Lunch | Games | Dinner/Play | Go to bed | Night |

Midnight to noon   **Noon to midnight**

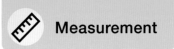
Hours

The 12 hours measured on a clock can stand for both the hours from 12 o'clock midnight to 12 o'clock noon, and the hours from 12 o'clock noon to 12 o'clock midnight.

The **short hand** moves around the clock to measure how many **hours** have passed. When the short hand points to 7, it tells you that it is **7 o'clock**.

It takes **5 minutes** for the long hand to move from one of the hour numbers to the next.

Minutes

Minutes are smaller units of time than hours. There are 60 minutes in 1 hour. Minutes can be shown by lines around the edge of a clock.

The **long hand** moves around the clock to measure how many minutes have passed.

It takes **1 minute** for the long hand to move from one line to the next.

Digital clocks

You will also see clocks that show the time simply as numbers. Look at these two clocks. Both tell you that it is 10 o'clock.

10:00

Days, weeks, and months

There are **24 hours** in a day, and a grouping of **7 days** is called a week. Days are also grouped into larger units of time that we call months. There are **12 months** in a year.

Calendars

A calendar is a type of chart or table. Each month usually has its own chart showing the days and weeks in that month. Calendars can help us plan when to do things.

Saturday and Sunday are called the weekend.

October

Monday	Tuesday	Wednesday	Thursday	Friday	Saturday	Sunday
				1	2	3
4	5 Swimming	6	7 Piano lesson	8 My birthday!	9 My party!	10
11	12	13	14	15	16 Soccer practice	17
18	19 Swimming	20	21	22	23	24 Grandpa's birthday
25	26	27	28 Piano lesson	29	30	31

7 days make 1 week.

How many days in a month?

Most months have 31 days, but 4 months—April, June, September, and November—only have 30 days. February, however, is a very unusual month. Most years it has just 28 days, but every 4 years it gains an extra day. A year with a 29-day February is called a **leap year**.

Month line

To help us remember how many months equals 1 year, and the order the months occur in, we can show them on a number line.

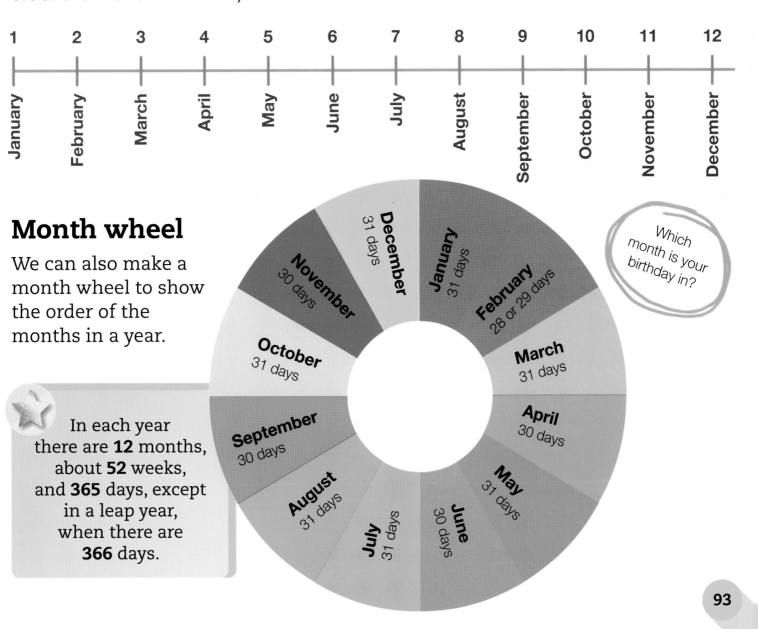

1	2	3	4	5	6	7	8	9	10	11	12
January	February	March	April	May	June	July	August	September	October	November	December

Month wheel

We can also make a month wheel to show the order of the months in a year.

Which month is your birthday in?

⭐ In each year there are **12** months, about **52** weeks, and **365** days, except in a leap year, when there are **366** days.

December 31 days
January 31 days
February 28 or 29 days
March 31 days
April 30 days
May 31 days
June 30 days
July 31 days
August 31 days
September 30 days
October 31 days
November 30 days

Temperature

We measure temperature, or how hot or cold something is, using a tool called a **thermometer**. It is useful to know what the temperature of something or somewhere is, because it can affect what we do and what we wear.

Temperature units

The units of measurement for temperature are called **degrees**. There are several different types of degrees, but most people use **degrees Fahrenheit (°F)** or **degrees Celsius (°C)**.

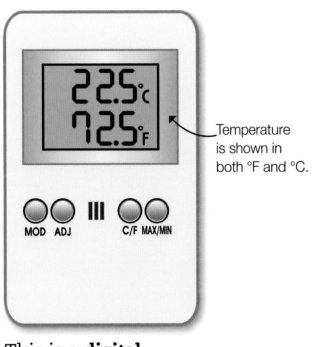

This is a **digital thermometer**. The display tells us the temperature.

Temperature is shown in both °F and °C.

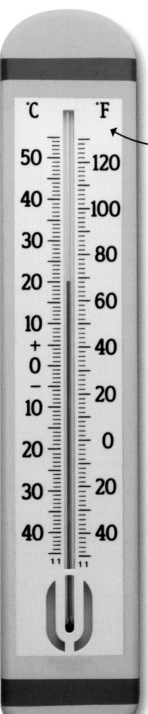

Many analogue thermometers show temperature in both °F and °C.

This is an **analogue thermometer**. The height of the blue liquid in the tiny tube tells us the temperature. Look carefully to see what number it has reached.

A healthy human being will have a body temperature of about **98°F** or **37°C**.

86°F (30°C)

If it was **86°F** or **30°C**, you would feel **hot**.

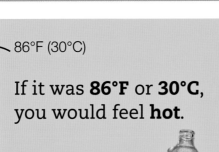

If it was **41°F** or **5°C**, you would feel **cold**.

41°F (5°C)

68°F (20°C)

If it was **68°F** or **20°C**, you would feel **comfortable**.

Money

We use money to pay for things that we need or want. The amount of money we pay for something is measured in **units**, such as **dollars ($)**.

Using an app on a phone

Spending money
There are many different ways of paying for things.

Using coins and bills

Visiting an ATM

Using checks

Exact amounts and change

When we use **bank cards, apps** on phones, and **checks**, we give someone the **exact amount** of money for the things we are buying.

For example, when Mia's dad pays $30 for their meal using his bank card, the card machine takes exactly $30 from his bank account.

Change

We can also use **coins** and **bills** to pay for something.

If we don't have the right coins and bills to equal the exact cost of what we're buying, we use bills or coins that are worth more.

Then the person we pay will have to give us some money back. This money is called **change**.

When we pay with bills, we often get our change in coins.

Using coins

Coins are a type of money. There are different types of coins, each with its own **value**. The value of a coin is marked on it.

Instead of writing **cent**, we shorten it to **¢**.

1¢

This coin is called a penny. Its value is 1 cent. It is the lowest-value coin we use.

This coin is called a nickle. Its value is 5 cents.

5¢

100 cents has the same value as 1 dollar, or **$1**. As well as coins, we use **bills** as money. They have higher values, such as $10 and $50.

Worth the same

One coin may be worth the same amount as several coins of less value.

If you want buy something that costs 5¢, but don't have a nickle, you can use five pennies instead.

1¢ + 1¢ + 1¢ + 1¢ + 1¢ = 5¢

If you want to buy something that costs 6¢, you can use one of these 2 different combinations, or groups, of coins.

5¢ + 1¢ = 6¢

or

1¢ + 1¢ + 1¢ + 1¢ + 1¢ + 1¢ = 6¢

Here are two different combinations of coins that we can use to pay for something that costs 10¢.

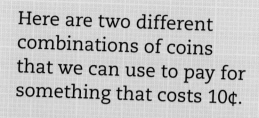 + 5¢ = 10¢

or

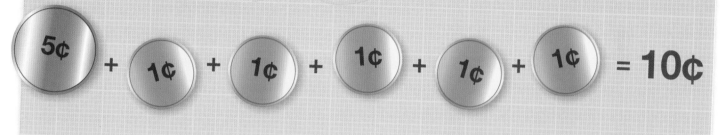

5¢ + 1¢ + 1¢ + 1¢ + 1¢ + 1¢ = 10¢

You can also use bars to show how these 2 different groups of coins are worth the same amount.

5¢
5¢

5¢ + 5¢ = 10¢

2 nickles have a total value of 10¢.

5¢

| 1¢ | 1¢ | 1¢ | 1¢ | 1¢ |

5¢ + 1¢ + 1¢ + 1¢ + 1¢ + 1¢ = 10¢

1 nickle plus 5 pennies have a total value of 10¢.

Spending money

You'll need to use many of the different math skills that you've learned when you go shopping.

Buying items

Imagine we buy 3 items of clothing: a T-shirt, a baseball cap, and a pair of socks. Let's find the total cost.

The price tag tells us how much money each item costs.

Money math

When you spend money, you may use these math skills:

• **Addition** to add prices together and figure out how much you've spent.

• **Subtraction** to figure out if you will have any change.

• **Multiplication** to figure out the total cost if you're buying more than one of something.

• **Division** to figure out how many of something you can buy with the money you have.

• **Number lines** to figure out how much change you'll get.

$6

$3

$2

We can show the total cost of the items on ten frames. Each mini item stands for $1.

Each filled square of the ten frames stands for $1.

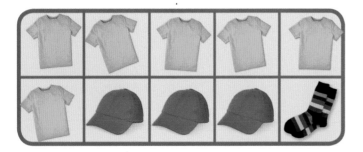

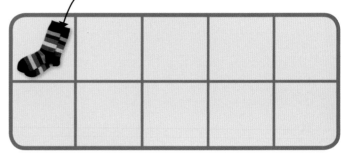

$10 + $1 = $11

Getting change

Let's say we pay $11 for the clothes with a $20 bill. By using 2 ten frames (which make 20) to stand for the $20 bill, we can figure out how much change we get back. We fill the second ten frame with counters to give us the answer.

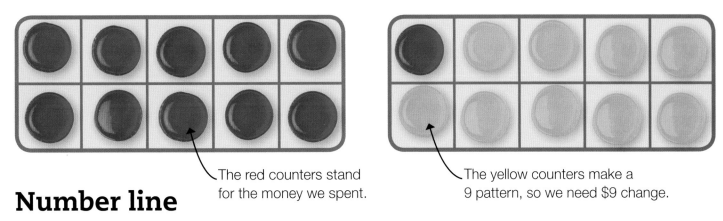

The red counters stand for the money we spent.

The yellow counters make a 9 pattern, so we need $9 change.

Number line

We can also show the money we spent on the clothes, and the change from $20, on a number line.

This part of the number line shows the $11 we spent on clothes.

This part of the number line shows the $9 change from the $20 bill.

0 1 2 3 4 5 6 7 8 9 10 11 12 13 14 15 16 17 18 19 20

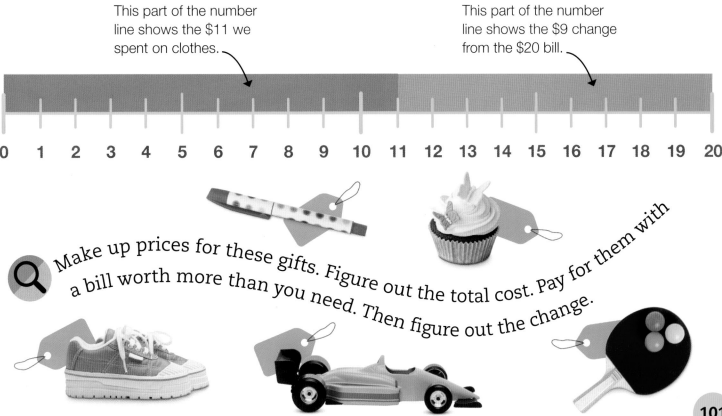

Make up prices for these gifts. Figure out the total cost. Pay for them with a bill worth more than you need. Then figure out the change.

Shapes

Everything has a shape. We give some shapes names that are based on the way they look.

You can see shapes all around you! Try naming them (see pages 104 and 107).

Noticing shapes

When we notice what a shape looks like, we are talking about the shape's **properties**. Looking at a shape's properties helps us see how a shape is similar to or different from other shapes.

Vertex

Face

Edge

Properties of shapes

Let's look at some common properties of shapes.

Face
A face is a flat surface of a shape. Curved surfaces are not faces.

Edge
An edge is where two surfaces meet. Edges can be straight or curved.

Vertex
A vertex is a point, or corner, where two or more edges meet. The plural of vertex is **vertices**.

Edge

Curved surface

Look at the shapes of objects around your home. Can you point to their faces, edges, and vertices?

Angles

Another important property of shapes is their **angles**. You'll find the angles of a shape at the vertices.

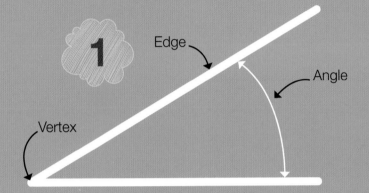

1 Edge · Angle · Vertex

Here there is only a small angle, or turn, between the two edges.

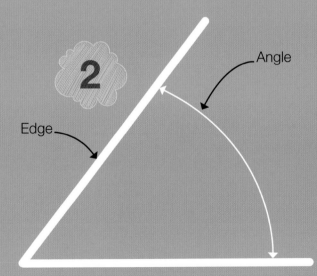

2 Edge · Angle

Here the edges have moved farther apart, creating a bigger angle.

3 We mark a right angle with straight lines like this.

This angle is called a **right angle**. It measures exactly **90°**.

Look at a cereal box, like the one on the opposite page. Point to where the angles are. Are they right angles?

2-D shapes

Some shapes are flat. This means that they have **length** and **height**, but no depth or thickness. We say that these shapes are **two-dimensional**, which is usually shortened to **2-D**.

Different 2-D shapes

Here are some 2-D shapes that you should learn to recognize and name. You could practice looking for them in objects around you at home or at school.

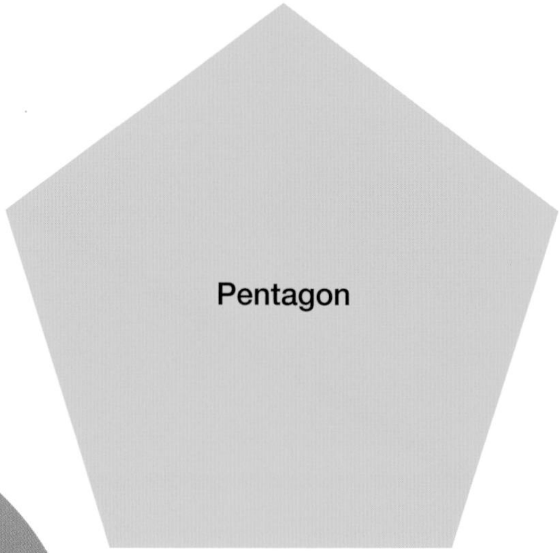

Pentagon

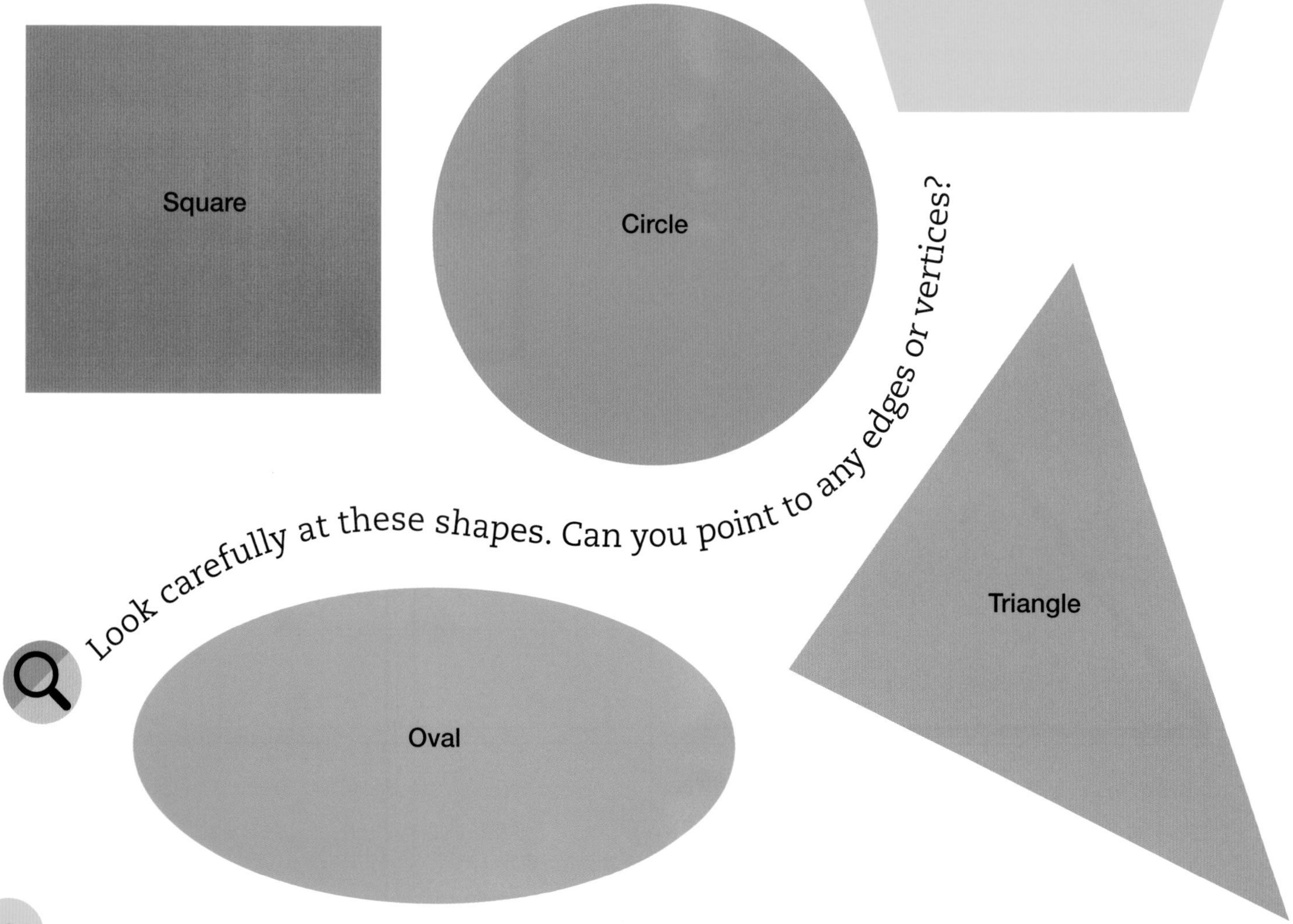

Square

Circle

Look carefully at these shapes. Can you point to any edges or vertices?

Oval

Triangle

Polygons

2-D shapes may have straight or curved edges, or a mixture of both. But when a 2-D shape has only straight edges, it belongs to a group of shapes called **polygons**. Here are some common polygons, with their properties.

A rectangle is a shape with 4 right angles. A **square** is a type of rectangle.

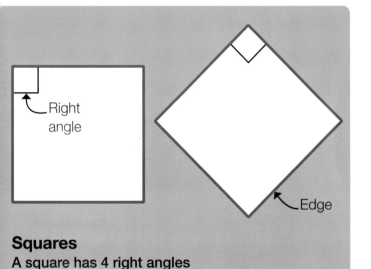

Squares
A square has 4 right angles and 4 edges, or sides, of equal length.

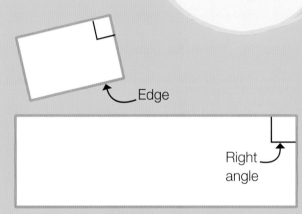

Rectangles
A rectangle has 4 right angles and 4 edges, or sides. Opposite sides are of equal length, but one pair of sides can be longer than the other.

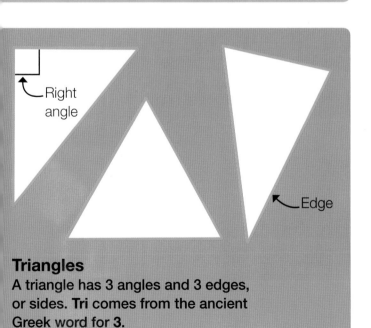

Triangles
A triangle has 3 angles and 3 edges, or sides. **Tri** comes from the ancient Greek word for **3**.

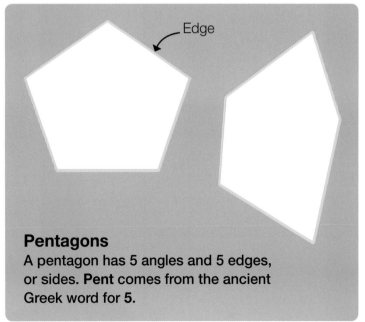

Pentagons
A pentagon has 5 angles and 5 edges, or sides. **Pent** comes from the ancient Greek word for **5**.

3-D shapes

Some shapes have **length**, **height**, and **depth**. They are called **three-dimensional** or **3-D** shapes. Cubes, cones, and pyramids are all examples of 3-D shapes.

Looking for 3-D shapes

There are 3-D shapes all around you. Let's look at these two 3-D shapes. Then make a note of any objects you see that are the same shape as these.

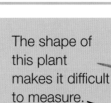

The shape of this plant makes it difficult to measure.

Tricky shapes

Any shape that has length, height, and depth is 3-D. Even a complicated shape, such as this plant in a pot, is 3-D.

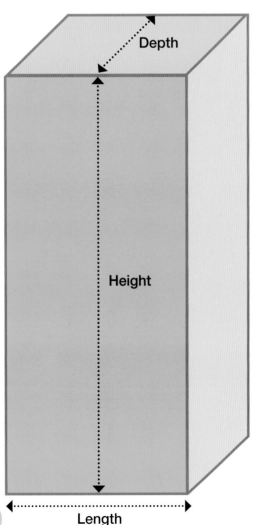

Depth

Height

Length

This red shape has 3 dimensions: length, height, and depth. It could be the shape of a box of cookies, a closet, or even a very tall building.

3-D shapes can be **solid**, like a wooden block, or **empty inside**, like a box.

This is a 3-D shape, too. Cans of food are usually this shape. Toilet-paper rolls are also this shape.

Common 3-D shapes

We also group 3-D shapes into types, based on their properties.
Here are some of the most common types of 3-D shapes.

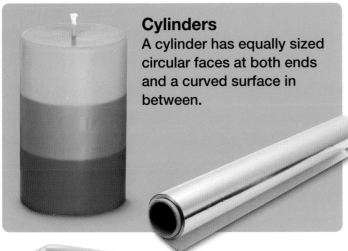

Cylinders
A cylinder has equally sized circular faces at both ends and a curved surface in between.

Cones
A cone has a circular base and a curved surface. It's like a cylinder, but the curved surface narrows to a point, or vertex.

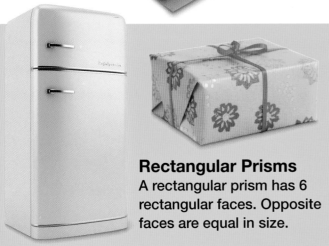

Rectangular Prisms
A rectangular prism has 6 rectangular faces. Opposite faces are equal in size.

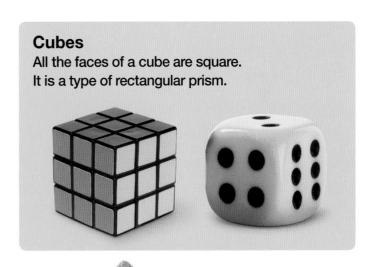

Cubes
All the faces of a cube are square.
It is a type of rectangular prism.

Pyramids
A pyramid has triangular faces with a vertex at the top and a base that can be a triangle, square, or another polygon (see page 105). The ancient pyramids in Egypt are enormous examples of this shape.

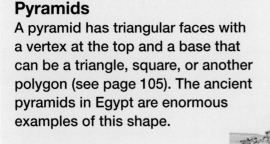

Nets of shapes

A net is a flat 2-D shape that can be folded up and stuck together to make a 3-D shape.

Net of a cube

This flat shape is a net of a cube. You can see that it is made up of 6 squares.

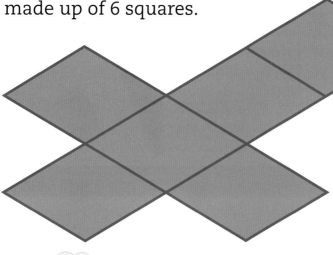

This end square will be the lid.

Edge

1 The 6 squares can be folded up and stuck together to make a cube.

2 When you fold the shape along the lines, they form the edges of the cube.

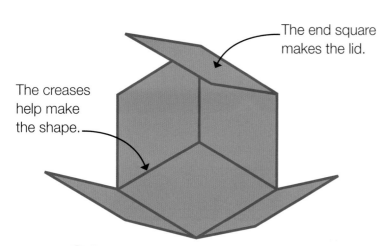

The end square makes the lid.

The creases help make the shape.

3 The squares that surround the central square become the cube's sides.

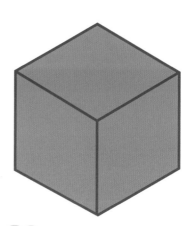

4 The flat net shape has been turned into a cube.

More nets

Here are 4 more flat shapes that can be folded up to make 3-D shapes.

Cone
The net of a cone is a circle connected to a curved shape.

The circle forms the base of the cone.

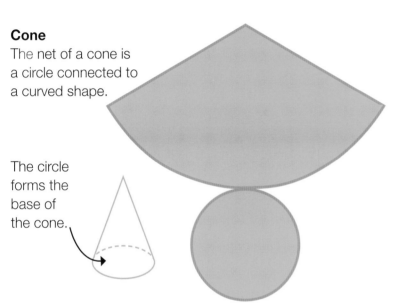

Rectangular Prism
This net of a rectangular prism is made up of 6 rectangles of 2 different sizes.

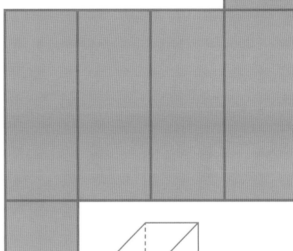

The opposite faces are equal.

The 4 triangles meet at a point, or vertex, at the top.

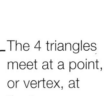

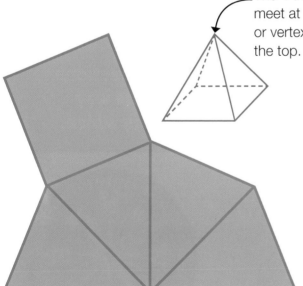

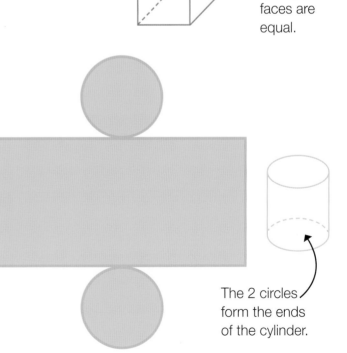

The 2 circles form the ends of the cylinder.

Square-based pyramid
A square and 4 triangles form the net of a square-based pyramid.

Cylinder
A cylinder's net is formed from 2 circles and a rectangle.

Direction

Direction is about where something is moving toward or pointing to. **Left**, **right**, and **straight** are directions. Points on a **compass**, such as **north**, are also directions. Ways of **turning**, such as **clockwise**, are directions too.

Left, right, and straight

The directions **left**, **right**, and **straight** can be used to tell someone which way to go to get somewhere.

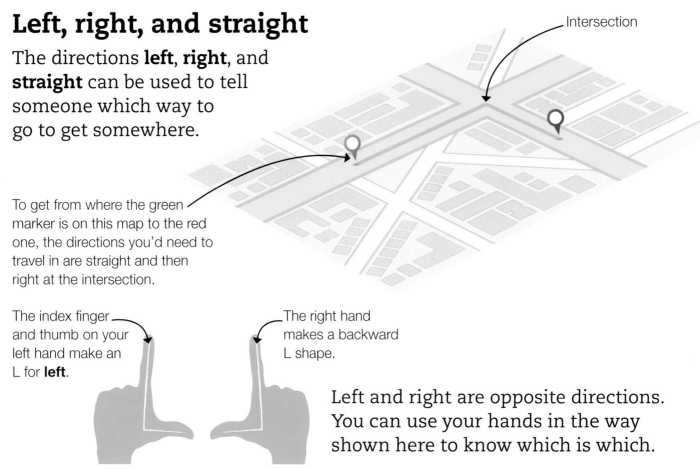

Intersection

To get from where the green marker is on this map to the red one, the directions you'd need to travel in are straight and then right at the intersection.

The index finger and thumb on your left hand make an L for **left**.

The right hand makes a backward L shape.

Left and right are opposite directions. You can use your hands in the way shown here to know which is which.

Compass points

A compass is a tool we use to find out where a place is and which direction to go to get there. It shows the directions **north**, **south**, **east**, and **west**, and also directions in between.

This compass shows these directions as N, E, S, and W.

Clockwise

The hands on a clock turn in one direction. We call this direction **clockwise**. It's the same as turning, or rotating, to the right. We call turning in the opposite direction, or to the left, **counterclockwise**.

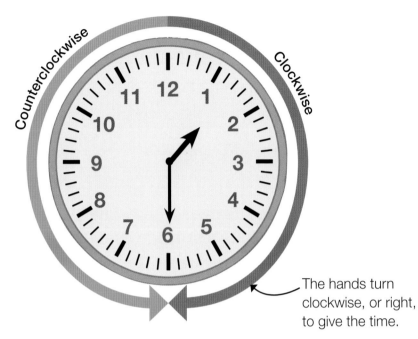

The hands turn clockwise, or right, to give the time.

Turns

The pink areas of the clocks below show different **turns**.

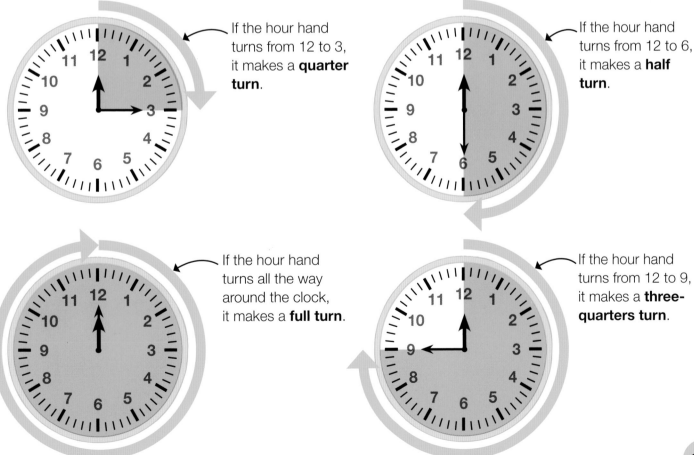

If the hour hand turns from 12 to 3, it makes a **quarter turn**.

If the hour hand turns from 12 to 6, it makes a **half turn**.

If the hour hand turns all the way around the clock, it makes a **full turn**.

If the hour hand turns from 12 to 9, it makes a **three-quarters turn**.

Reflection of objects

When you see yourself in a mirror, what you see is called a reflection. Your reflection looks exactly like you do, but it has been flipped around from left to right.

More about reflection

When things are reflected, they may also be flipped from top to bottom, such as these balloons over a lake. The place where the reflection starts, in this case at the lake's surface, is called the mirror line.

Objects are reflected across a mirror line.

The reflection looks the same, but it has been flipped from top to bottom, so the basket is at the top of the balloon.

Symmetry

We can draw a line through the middle of some shapes so that each half is like a reflection of the other. We describe shapes like this as **symmetrical**. The line dividing the two halves is called the **line of symmetry**.

Not all shapes have lines of symmetry. Shapes without them are called **asymmetrical**.

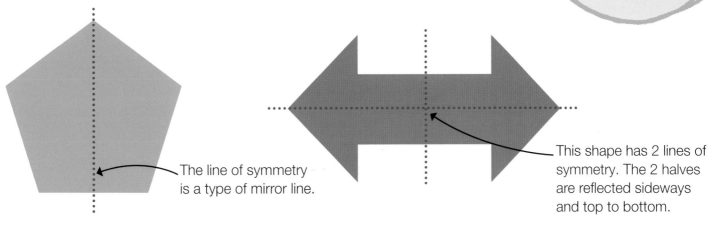

The line of symmetry is a type of mirror line.

This shape has 2 lines of symmetry. The 2 halves are reflected sideways and top to bottom.

Try it!

Many things around us can be divided into two halves by a line of symmetry. Find a small mirror and place it along the dotted line in these half pictures. Now you should see the complete picture.

Collecting data

We can find information, called data, about lots of different things. To collect data, we ask questions and write down what we find out.

How do we collect data?

Before we collect data, we need to think of what we want to find out. Imagine that in your class at school you want to find out which month has the most birthdays. These are the steps you might take:

Months

January
February
March
April
May
June
July
August
September
October
November
December

Make a list of the months of the year.

Make a list of all the children in the class, to make sure you don't miss anyone.

Class list

NAME
Jacob
Emma
Peter
Lucas
Tom
Erik
Zoe
Ruby
Katy
Ambika

Ask each child on the class list which month their birthday falls in. Put a tally mark beside that month on your months list.

Tally marks

We use tally marks to write down how many things we have counted when collecting data (see page 22). You make one tally mark for each thing that you count.

Each mark means 1.

This group of marks means 5.

Birthdays in each month

Months of the year	Number of children
January	¦ ¦ ¦
February	¦ ¦
March	卅 ¦ ¦
April	卅 ¦
May	¦
June	¦ ¦
July	卅
August	¦ ¦
September	¦
October	¦ ¦
November	¦ ¦
December	¦

A mark for each child is placed next to their birthday month.

From the tally marks, you can see how many birthdays there are in each month. For example, 5 children had birthdays in March.

April is the month with the most birthdays.

Showing data

Once you have gathered your data, you can then show it, on paper or a screen, in a way that helps you see the information it contains clearly.

How to show data

You can use words, numbers, or even pictures to show the data that you have gathered. The graphs and tables shown here are some of the most popular ways of showing data, so that it is quick and easy to understand.

 Look at the pictogram on the right. You can easily see that oranges are the most popular fruit and bananas the least.

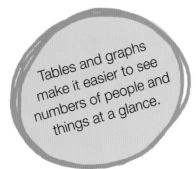
Tables and graphs make it easier to see numbers of people and things at a glance.

Pictograms

A pictogram is a chart that shows data in the form of pictures. This pictogram tells us about the types of fruit a group of children like best. To learn more about pictograms, see pages 118–119.

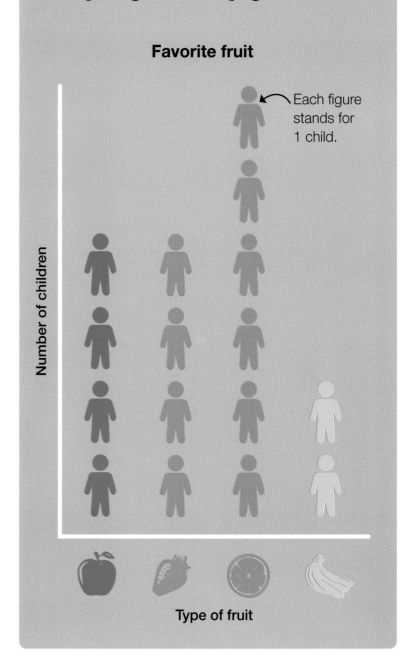

Favorite fruit

Each figure stands for 1 child.

Number of children

Type of fruit

116

Bar graphs

In the graph below, you can see that each bar stands for the number of children who prefer a particular type of vegetable. Can you see that peas are the most popular vegetable and carrots the least popular? For more on bar graphs, see pages 120–121.

The numbers at the side tell you how many children there are.

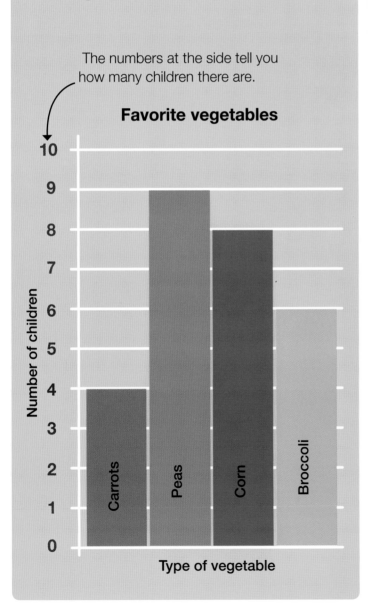

Favorite vegetables

Tables

The table below shows the prices of different drinks and snacks in a café. It is split into columns to show three different sizes. Can you see that a large soup is the most expensive thing and a small apple the cheapest?

These headings tell you the size of the food or drink.

Food and drink prices

	Small	Medium	Large
Tea	$1	$1.20	$1.50
Coffee	$1.25	$1.50	$1.85
Orange	35¢	55¢	75¢
Apple	30¢	50¢	70¢
Banana	35¢	55¢	75¢
Cake	$1.30	$1.60	$1.90
Cookies	50¢	75¢	$1.00
Chips	50¢	90¢	$1.50
Soup	$1.00	$1.50	$2.50

These headings tell you what the food or drink is.

Pictograms

You've seen (on page 116) that pictograms use small pictures to show data. The pictures are usually placed side by side in rows, or up and down in columns.

Making a pictogram

In this pictogram, the pictures are arranged in rows. You can see that the pictures are carefully lined up with each other so that it is easier for you to compare.

This is the title—it tells you what the pictogram is showing.

Each figure represents 1 child. This is shown in the key.

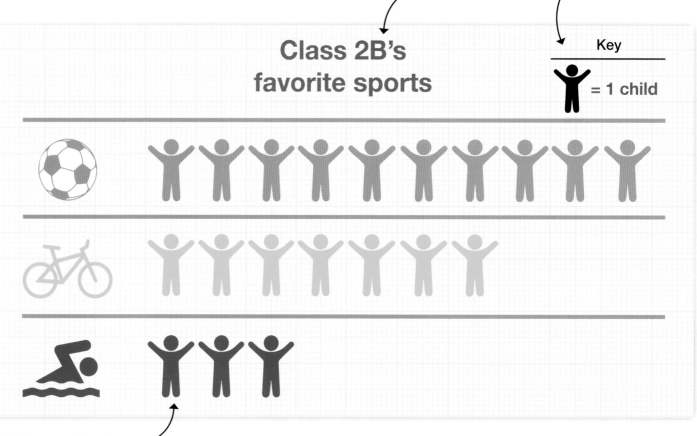

Make sure that the pictures line up.

Can you see that soccer is the most popular sport in Class 2B?

Larger amounts

When a pictogram shows larger numbers or amounts, each picture may stand for more than 1 thing. Here, there is 1 bird picture for every 2 real-life birds.

Always look at the **key** on a pictogram to check how many things each picture stands for.

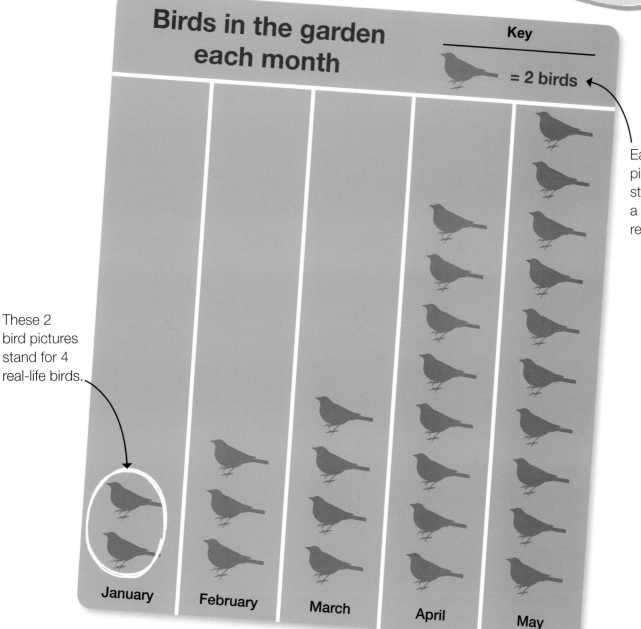

Birds in the garden each month

Key

= 2 birds

Each bird picture stands for a group of 2 real-life birds.

These 2 bird pictures stand for 4 real-life birds.

January   February   March   April   May

Can you see that 8 birds (4 groups of 2) visited the garden in March?

Bar graphs

Bar graphs show data using bars (see page 117). The bars can be arranged side by side or one above the other. The height or length of a bar shows the amount it stands for.

Making a bar graph

On page 115, tally marks were used to show the birthdays in each month for a class of children. Look below to see how this data has been made into a bar graph.

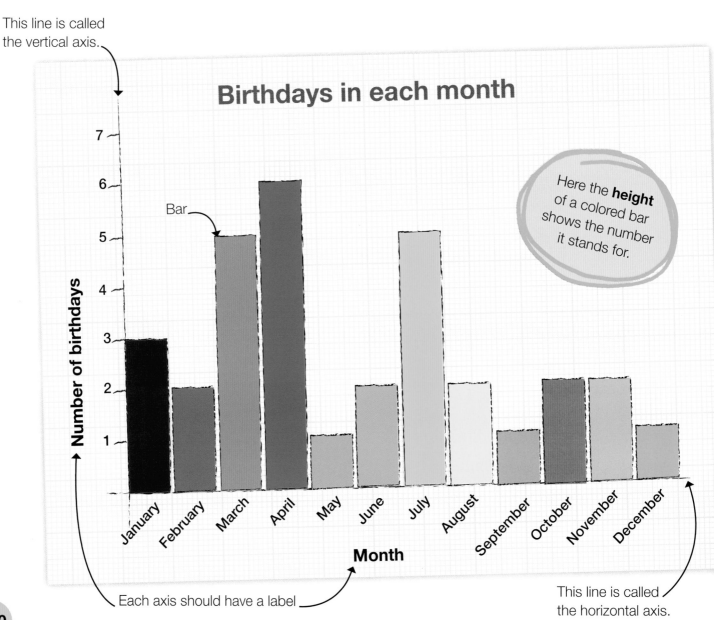

This line is called the vertical axis.

Bar

Here the **height** of a colored bar shows the number it stands for.

Birthdays in each month

Number of birthdays

Month

Each axis should have a label

This line is called the horizontal axis.

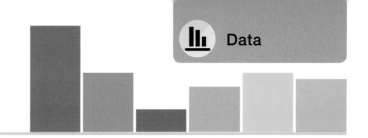
Using different data

We can collect data on all kinds of things. You could ask everyone in your class if they have a pet, and what it is. Then you could put this data on a bar graph to see what type of pet is the most popular.

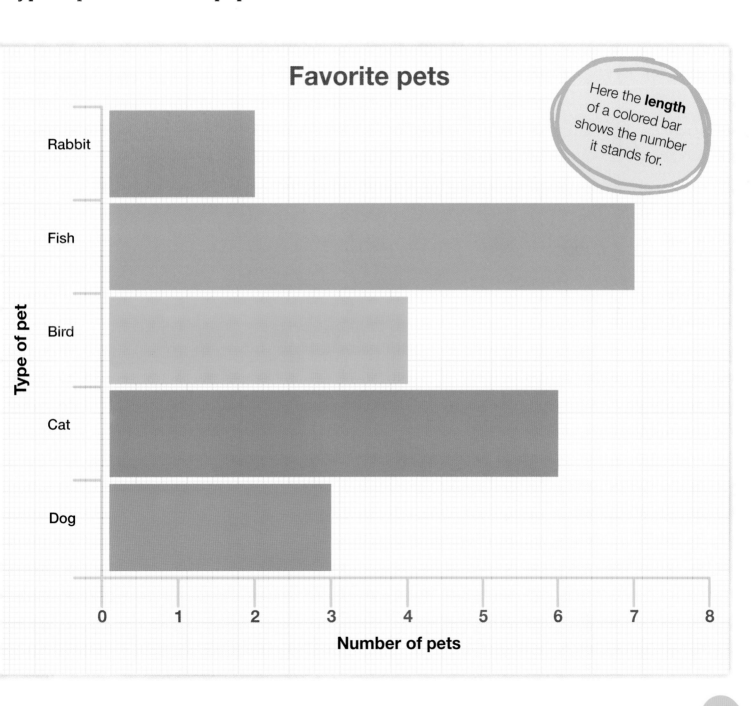

Favorite pets

Here the **length** of a colored bar shows the number it stands for.

Type of pet

Rabbit
Fish
Bird
Cat
Dog

Number of pets
0 1 2 3 4 5 6 7 8

Glossary

100s chart Square grid made up of 100 small squares in rows and columns of 10. The small squares are often numbered from 1 to 100

Add To join numbers or amounts together. We use the symbol "+" to mean added to, or plus

Analogue Describes a clock with moving hands to show the time, or a thermometer with a scale on it to show temperature

Angle Area formed by two lines that meet at a vertex, or corner. Angles are measured in degrees (°)

Array Arrangement of objects in a pattern with equal rows and equal columns

Asymmetry When a shape does not have perfectly matching halves. Opposite of symmetry

Bar Rectangle used to show an amount of something or a measurement, such as a length

Calculation Process of figuring out the answer to a math problem

Calendar Table, or collection of tables, that shows the days, weeks, and months of a year

Compare To look at how things or amounts are different or similar

Compass Tool used to find directions, such as north and south

Data Collection of facts, numbers, or other information

Degree Unit for measuring angles; unit for measuring temperature. The symbol for degrees is " ° "

Digits Symbols we use to write numbers. They are 0, 1 2, 3, 4, 5, 6, 7, 8, and 9

Digital Describes a clock or thermometer that shows the time or temperature with just numbers

Dimension Another word for a measure of size, such as length, depth, and height

Divide To split an amount into smaller, equal amounts. We use the symbol "÷" to mean divided by

Edge Side of a 2-D shape or where two faces of a 3-D shape meet

Estimate To give an idea of an amount that has not been measured or counted exactly

Even number Number that can be divided exactly by 2

Face Flat surface of a 3-D shape

Fraction Part of a whole amount or number

Grid Horizontal and vertical lines that cross to make a network of small rectangles

Half One part of two equal parts that make up a whole amount

Mass How much something weighs

Measure To find the exact amount or size of something

Multiple The number that results when you multiply numbers together

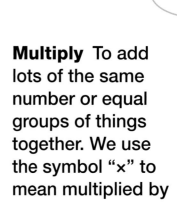

Multiply To add lots of the same number or equal groups of things together. We use the symbol "×" to mean multiplied by

Net Flat shape that can be folded to make a 3-D shape

Number line Line marked with equally spaced numbers, used for counting and calculating

Glossary

Odd number Number that cannot be divided exactly by 2

Pattern Ordered arrangement of numbers and objects

Polygon 2-D shape with three or more edges

Protractor Tool used to draw and measure angles

Plus Name for the addition symbol "+"

Scale Equally spaced markings, often numbered on a line, that appear on measuring devices such as rulers or thermometers

Subtract To take away. We use the symbol "–" to mean take away, or minus

Symmetry When a shape has two perfectly matching halves

Tally Way of counting in groups of five, using marks to stand for each item

Temperature Measure of how hot or cold something is

Ten frame Grid with ten squares in two rows of five squares, used for learning to count and calculate

Times table Chart showing the numbers we make when we multiply, or times, a number by 1, 2, 3, 4, 5, and so on. Also called multiplication table

Vertex Point where two or more lines, or edges, meet to form an angle, or corner

Whole number Numbers made of digits, including 0, but with no fractions

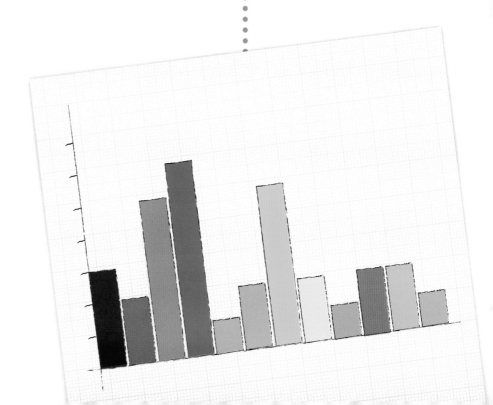

More useful math words

Here are a few more math words that you may come across as you continue to explore the amazing world of math.

Commutative Used to describe adding and multiplying, in which the answer is the same no matter what order the numbers are added or multiplied in.

Efficient Better or easier way of doing something

Equivalent Equal in value

Inverse Opposite of something. Multiplying is the inverse of dividing

Numeral Number, such as 6, 7, or 100, written with one or more digits

Represent To stand for, show, or mean. We can use counters and bars to represent people, objects, and measurements

Subitize To see the total amount of a group of things without counting them one by one

Index

Acknowledgments

DORLING KINDERSLEY would like to thank the following: Gareth Lowe and Mike Ollerton for fact checking, Jim Green for design assistance, Lizzie Davey for additional editorial work, Polly Goodman for proofreading, Helen Peters for indexing, and Sakshi Saluja for picture research.